Love, Sorrow, and Rage

Destitut
*Manhat**ice*

Love, Sorrow, and Rage

Destitute Women in a
Manhattan Residence

Alisse Waterston

Temple University Press
Philadelphia

Temple University Press, Philadelphia 19122
Copyright © 1999 by Temple University
All right reserved
Published 1999
Printed in the United States of America

⊗ The paper used in this publication meets the requirements of
American National Standard for Information Sciences–Permanence
of Paper for Printed Library Materials, ANSI Z39.48-1984

Library of Congress Cataloging-in-Publication Data

Waterston, Alisse, 1951–
    Love, sorrow, and rage : destitute women in a Manhattan residence
/ Alisse Waterston.
        p.   cm.
    Includes bibliographical references and index.
    ISBN 1-56639-706-5 (cloth : alk. paper) – ISBN 1-56639-707-3
(pbk. : alk. paper)
        1. Homeless women–New York (State)–New York–Social conditions.
2. Poor women–New York (State)–New York–Social conditions.
I. Title.
HV4506.N6W37   1999
362.83′086′942–dc21   98-32269
                                                         CIP

To Herlene Lawton
with love and respect

Contents

Acknowledgments

I AM DEEPLY grateful to many people from different parts of my life who have nurtured and nourished me, and so this book. I thank the women of Woodhouse first, for it is from them I have learned so much about being open to love and caring, about the deepest of sorrows, and about the power of rage. I hope my attempt to capture their words and the courage of their lives does some justice to the faith they have shown in me.

I wish to thank my husband, Howard, whose love is my special treasure, and whose friendship and faith sustain me daily.

My gratitude also extends to my mentors and colleagues at the HIV Center for Clinical and Behavioral Research of Columbia University, which supported this project. In particular, my thanks go to Ezra Susser, Zena Stein, Bob Kertzner, Anke Ehrhardt, Alan Berkman, Joyce Hunter, Wanda Grant, Helga Saez, and Kostas Gounis. For their insights and encouragement, I thank anthropologists Ida Susser, Pat Antoniello, Paul Farmer, Joan Cassell, and Mary Anglin. I also thank David Maynard for his thoughtful comments on an early draft of the manuscript, and Dave's student Susan Jarvis, who served as my summer research assistant.

Special thanks go to Terry Williams, my colleague and my good friend for life, who is always helpful and encouraging. I also appreciate many students at the New School for Social Research, who provided helpful commentary on this work.

I deeply appreciate Michael Ames of Temple University Press, who so ably provides gracious support and the best editorial advice all at once. I thank Temple University Press reviewer Gwendolyn Dordick, and one anonymous reviewer, for providing helpful critique of the manuscript. For their warm support and careful attention to this work, I thank Jenny French, production coordinator, and Bobbe Needham, copy editor.

The staff and administration at Woodhouse deserve special acknowledgment for providing me unhindered access to the community residence, and for allowing me to interact with the women of Woodhouse as I saw fit. For their camaraderie, I give many thanks to my colleagues at Surveys Unlimited/Horowitz Associates: Elvira Luzbet Gerena, Marivel Gomez, Anita Holmes, Darren Leib, Linda Levine, Nuria Riera, and Yihan Xie.

I want to express appreciation to my closest family and friends for their love, patience, and support. I especially thank my mother, Louise Waterston, my best friend, Claudia Brandt Arioli, and my children, Matthew Zuckerman and Leah Horowitz, for their special understanding about the importance of this work to me. I extend special thanks to Sidney and Elaine Horowitz, Adrienne Waterston, David Breindel, and David Waterston, my brother and photographer. To my "prima politica," Virginia Schofield, I thank you so much for gracing the cover of my book with your painting; how happy I am that our works of the heart are presented here as one.* Finally, I thank my friend Herlene Lawton for her insights, her friendship, her trust. I dedicate this book to Herlene, with love and respect.

*Virginia Schofield is a Cuban-American painter working in Washington, D.C. She studied at American University and the Washington Studio School and has exhibited widely.

Prologue

An Urban Ethnography for Our Times

Sketching Love, Sorrow, and Rage

This is a story about a group of poor women who live in Woodhouse, one of dozens of facilities designed to provide housing and other services for the destitute in New York City. Their life stories unfold as I sit with them at a kitchen table, preparing meals, talking, sharing intimacies. In this setting, we hear from women like Nora Gaines, Hattie McFarrell, and Dixie Register about what it is like to live on the street and how it feels to lose your mind, about the taste of crack cocaine and the sweetness of friendship.

Some might consider this an unpopular subject—no one wants to know about poor women, they think, and no one wants to read about poor women. I strongly disagree. In various guises, the general topic of this book gets front page coverage in daily newspapers and magazines across the country: the growing gap between rich and poor in America, inner-city crime, problems of welfare "dependency," drug addiction, and the spread of AIDS. This coverage and the debate it raises reflect a yearning to understand, to explain, and to solve the human crisis that surrounds us.

1

And it will not go away. In fact, we will be hearing more and more about poor women as welfare "reform" is implemented state by state, bringing with it more poverty, more homelessness, more social suffering.[1]

I have written this book to challenge all of us to look at the ways in which our society and the workings of our political, economic and popular culture contribute to the suffering experienced by our most vulnerable citizens. Historically, politicians and the media as well as social scientists have distorted findings regarding vulnerable populations; the politics of the day promise to follow this tradition. I am compelled by an ongoing politic of "blaming the poor" to offer intimate portraits of the women and to reflect on political and economic processes that contextualize the lives of the women and the institution in which they reside.

In a specific sense, this book is based on more than two years of ethnographic research I conducted as part of a larger effort to develop an AIDS prevention program for a population identified as at high risk for infection.[2] In a broader sense, my personal and professional background has also been an important influence in fashioning my perspective on these social and political issues.[3]

However difficult it is to demonstrate the connections, *all* our individual life stories are linked to larger social and historical processes that are beyond the control of most people. This theoretical insight is central to this book, and to the social critique I offer in it. The women of Woodhouse are among those the tabloid press, popular politicians, and some social scientists suggest are "the undeserving and disreputable poor." They would have us believe that women like these are nothing more than victims of their own or their families' weaknesses and sloth–social burdens, with no clear productive role. In the popular imagination, such women are "street people," "mad women," "disease vectors," "whores," "dope fiend crack addicts and alcoholics," "the underclass"–all of them wretched, bizarre, and amoral. Added to this public image is a belief that, collectively, the women of Woodhouse make up some kind of poor people's subculture, imbued with exotic rituals and strange behavior.

The prevailing stereotypes of the poor constitute a collective cultural fiction–an ideology about the poor. This ideology serves a central purpose: to obscure structural inequality and to help maintain our existing social arrangements. The excluded, marginalized, and disvalued internalize the harsh messages directed at them. Ideology, a powerful mechanism by which social forces become embodied as individual experience, is a social and political project. Meanwhile, as personal identity becomes muddled with dehumanizing ideologies, human suffering only intensifies.

In many ways, the women of Woodhouse share with other Americans the most treasured and basic assumptions of our times. By way of ethnographic portraits of the women and through their own words, this book seeks to dispel myths and stereotypes about our "social problems" and "problem populations." The stories attest both to the personal and social complexity of their lives and show that the women are, for the most part, quite ordinary. Ironically, it is their very ordinariness, as well as their diversity, that opens the door to defying, then shattering, our assumptions.

Confronting Myth and the Circulation of False Images

Because "culture" has been called the special domain of anthropologists, I might be expected to analyze the lives and experiences of Woodhouse women in terms of culture or, more specifically, "their culture." How simple that would be. Many such analyses have been accomplished and, particularly when applied to troublesome social groups or "alien" societies, they leave us with what seems a satisfying explanation: these people are products of their cultures.

Of course, there is more than one form of cultural analysis. Yet the analytic concept most favorably received, at least when applied to inner-city people of the United States, has ignored years of criticism thrown its way (Valentine 1968; Leacock 1971; Stack 1974; Aschenbrenner 1975; Susser 1982; Williams 1988, 1992, 1994; Katz 1989; 1995; Reed 1991; Waterston 1993; di Leonardo 1994). Popularized in part by twentieth-century anthropologists, this notion sees cultures as "discrete, bounded entities," "value-saturated and timeless," "internally homogeneous and coherent units, each capable of producing its own worldview, its particular patterning of mind," and "uniform essences, replicated through time" (Schneider 1995:9-13). Applying this notion of culture to the subjects of this ethnography would lead me to offer up a label, such as "the subculture of ———," and an analysis that confuses explanation with behavior.

I might have some difficulty composing a befitting term, however. Would it be the subculture of "Woodhouse"? of "homeless women"? of "the mentally ill homeless"? The difficulty lies in determining the boundary of inclusive and exclusive traits. If a subculture is a discrete and bounded entity, what composes it? And what lies outside it?

Despite this dilemma, many before me have succeeded in identifying subcultures all across America. For example, who has not heard of the drug subculture, the underclass, or the culture of poverty (Glazer and Moynihan 1963; Becker 1964; Lewis 1966; Johnson 1980; Moynihan 1986; Jencks and Peterson 1991; Wilson 1987, 1989)? Also, don't we *just know* what constitutes those subcultures and *who* their members are?

I find it impossible to ignore the inadequacies and superficialities of the concept of culture used in this way. In addition to the shortcomings already noted, much seems to be missing. Where did the subculture come from? When did it come into being? Why did it show up in the particular places it appears? How does it keep going? According to the culturalist approach outlined here, one need go only as far as the subculture itself for answers. Critics consider this approach sophistry–an example of circular and specious reasoning.

If the culturalist explanation is so wrongheaded, why does it continue to enjoy popularity? Do so many journalists, policy makers, ordinary people, and scholars continue to fall for this fallacious explanation because it is deceptively beautiful and superficially plausible? A look at some implications that flow from this culturalist model might provide some insight.

First, it is important to say that the culturalist model works with other social forces to "construct" social groups (Blumer 1971; Stern 1984). Like everything else, scholarly practice does not operate in a vacuum but develops within and is responsive to the social and political context in which it operates (Schneider 1995:12). Following the culturalist model, the "scholarly" practice of naming, classifying, and defining facilitates building a social group on the basis of one or more things its members may have in common. Those one or more things may include just about anything: circumstance, behavior, skin color, geography, age, sexuality, and so on (Valentine 1968).

Once a line has been drawn around "the group," however

it is constituted, certain possibilities open up: constructing symbolic representations, political mobilization, psychological relief (identity and belonging), political and economic claims making, collective resistance, legitimization, visibility and voice, and nation building, any or all of which may be played out in various local and global arenas (Hobsbawm and Ranger 1983; Ignatieff 1993; Fraser and Gordon 1994; Khan 1995). As the line is drawn, so difference is enlarged, and the possibility of "an-other" also opens up (Gilman 1988).

This is not to say that difference is necessarily problematic, but the paradoxical uses to which difference is put in particular historical junctures and political situations call for exploration. In any given situation, multiple interpretations, competing definitions, and a myriad of interests are at work. If a pattern can be discerned across time, space, and place, perhaps it lies in the relationship between social location (access to material resources and power) and particular consequences of "difference." The more limited the access of a particular group to material resources and power, the greater the likelihood that difference will translate into harmful consequences for the group and its purported members. As Edward Said observes, "difference can become an ideological infection" (1995:105).

In the exaggeration of difference, the other is born, objectified, and perceived as exotic, strange, frightening. In powerful hands, ideologies about particular "others" have real and painful consequences, contributing to everyday oppression, stigmatization, and ethnic cleansing.

It is not difficult to see how the culturalist model outlined earlier contributes to the production and reproduction of particular "others." Its taxonomic objective in hand, the approach proceeds as if there is some external, objective reality "out there" to name and classify. This makes it a safe approach, for it works under the assumptions of and in tandem with mainstream ideologies and dominant institutional practices. Whether they do so deliberately or unreflectively, culturalists do not merely describe, they help construct "discourses of domination" and reproduce "hegemonic discursive frames," to borrow from a discussion between Yvonne Zylan and Nancy Fraser (Zylan 1996:515-16; Fraser 1996: 533). Here we have a clue as to its continuing popularity. It doesn't matter if it is wrong headed, it matters that it does not threaten.

Studies of urban poverty in the United States offer a case in point. Journalists and scholars of the culturalist ilk seem never to tire of presenting what di Leonardo calls "fake ethnography," distorted portraits of the poor in inner cities (1994:6). As David Maynard observed (in an electronic communication to me on December 18, 1995), these accounts "are made palatable to a range of middle class, mostly white, 'educated' audiences by exoticizing, pathologizing and racializing the inner city." From these portraits, we now have a vast store of "telling metaphors for the poor," mean stereotypes embraced by policy makers and the popular press (Williams 1994:166-70).

"Through the prism of underclass ideology," the pages of my ethnographic narrative are stories about former bag ladies, the mentally and physically diseased, bad mothers, crack addicts, alcoholics, prostitutes, government dependents, the racialized and undeserving poor (di Leonardo 1994:13). Captured in stereotype, the women of Woodhouse are emblematic of all our social problems. Any one of these "attributes" signals the pressing social problems of our day;

collected under one roof, they form its powerful symbol. Woodhouse women are the quintessential "other"; for them, difference has become an ideological infection. Focused as we are on the women of Woodhouse, we cannot see past them to discover, then oppose, social inequality and injustice.

Critics of the culturalist approach offer alternative methods of thinking about and interpreting the lives of the urban poor in U.S. cities. Standing outside the particularistic categories of current American political life, these alternatives cannot be tagged "liberal" or "conservative." Unlike the culturalist model, these approaches are not propositions characterized by elegance and parsimony, nor are they particularly palatable to mainstream audiences. Instead, complicated and messy, they require us to look hard at common sources of both wealth and well-being, of misery and suffering. In ways complicated and involved, these analyses challenge accepted and acceptable definitions of problems, seeking to connect human lives to larger systems and processes.

In a chapter titled "Connections," anthropologist Eric R. Wolf has written, "[T]he world of humankind constitutes a . . . totality of interconnected processes, and inquiries that disassemble this totality and then fail to reassemble it falsify reality. Concepts like . . . 'culture' name bits and threaten to turn names into things." Wolf then urges social scientists to investigate "wider linkages"–"'webs' or 'nets' of relations that connect actors in local social fields to a wider context" (Wolf 1982:3, 23, 385; also see Schneider 1995:7). Similarly, Leith Mullings argues for studies that examine "vertical links that connect the social groups studied to the larger society" and ask, "[H]ow are these groups embedded in the political economy of the wider society?" (1987:6).

"To connect" means that we reassemble the bits that have been disassembled. This is a difficult task, in large part because the practice of splintering is so common, it is hard to keep an eye on the bigger picture. "The manner in which knowledge and institutions are organized in the contemporary world," argue Kleinman, Das, and Lock, "reifies the fragmentation of [social phenomena] while casting a veil of misrecognition over the domain as a whole." They go on to ask, "[Is it] because if seen as a whole it would be too threatening?" (1996:xix–xx).

To concern ourselves with the political economy of the wider society suggests we focus on a feature of social life touched upon earlier: differential access to material resources and power. Today, this directs our attention to the dynamics of capitalism and to how relations of production and processes of capital accumulation are experienced in the inner city (Wolf 1982; Harvey 1989; Sassen 1991; Maynard 1995; Schneider 1995). "Contemporary North America," Jane Schneider writes, "is a corner of the world where capitalism flourishes as nowhere else" (1995:20). In a sense, capitalism is a glue that binds social actors to each other in relations marked by inequality.

These relations, as Wolf points out, "take clout to set up, clout to maintain, and clout to defend." This kind of power Wolf calls "structural power," one of four modes he delineates. Structural power "is power that structures the political economy. . . . [It] shapes the social field of action so as to render some kinds of behavior possible, while making others less possible or impossible" (1990:587). The other modes of power operate in relation to structural power; they are "power as an attribute of the person, as potency or capability," power "as the ability of an ego to impose its will on an alter, in social action, in interpersonal relations," and "[tactical or organizational] power that controls the settings in which people may show forth their potentialities and interact with others." These forms of power transpire in social interactions and are played out in institutional settings where the basic groupings of society are reproduced: the family, the neighborhood, the school, the workplace, the shelter, the streets, the community residence, the prison. Even though "the notion of structural power is useful precisely because it allows us to delineate how the forces of the world impinge upon the people we study," it remains the mode neglected in the most popular understanding of the urban poor (1990:587).

In our popular and political culture, personal responsibility is the theme of the day. Indeed, the new welfare law is titled "The Personal Responsibility and Work Opportunity Reconciliation Act of 1996" ("President Signs" 1996; Uchitelle 1997). But individuals are accountable and have "agency" only to the degree that their potentialities have been nourished and allowed expression (Wolf 1990:587). As the poor and working poor have been pushed deeper into the "inner city" by means of "structural power," "organizational" power is unleashed in various social institutions: the school system, the marketplace, the criminal justice system, health and mental health care systems, the housing system (including shelters and residences), the family. To talk about personal accountability without considering those external forces that rein it in is to place an impossible and unfair burden on the individual concerned.

Despite pervasive rhetoric about individual responsibility, many scholars are taking a closer look at "external forces," for instance, examining cities as "loci of capital accumulation and investment, as reservoirs of labor, and as nodes of intervention by the state" (Wolf 1982:423; Harvey 1973; 1985; Castells 1977; Sassen 1991). In a recent study, David Maynard shows that inner cities of the United States are "sites of intersecting circuits of national and global capital accumulation," and he specifies how "inner city people are themselves the loci of multiple circuits of capital accumulation." To illustrate, Woodhouse women are among those "inner city consumers" to whom "a variety of products are specifically targeted (clothing, shoes, tobacco, alcohol, drugs)"; they are also, as my own project represents, "objects of study by a substantial social science and urban social policy industry which provides employment for a large number of middle class academics" (Maynard 1995:1–2).

"These are most definitely not simply abstract structural processes and outcomes of capitalist inequalities," Maynard writes, "since they have complicated, direct and all too often painful effects on the daily lives of inner city people" (1995: 2). Such painful effects are the subject of a recent issue of the journal *Daedalus* devoted to the topic and referred to there as "social suffering": it "results from what political, economic and institutional power does to people, and reciprocally, from how these forms of power themselves influence responses to social problems" (Kleinman, Das, and Lock 1996:xi).

In one of the *Daedalus* essays, physician/anthropologist Paul Farmer describes social suffering among residents of Do Kay, a rural village in Haiti (1996:261–83). In presenting the life histories of two people, Acephie and Chouchou, Farmer has us taste suffering. Refusing to leave it at that, he makes clear these stories "illustrate some of the mechanisms through which large-scale social forces crystallize into the sharp, hard surfaces of individual suffering" (1996: 263; 1992; 1994). Structural power is at play, limiting, constraining, confining "power of the person" (Wolf 1990:587). Farmer asks, "By what mechanisms do social forces become embodied as individual experience?" (1996:261–62). As I reflect on the lives of the women of Woodhouse, I believe the answer, in part, lies in the way in which poor people internalize dominant images and negative stereotypes in the course of their everyday experiences.

I do not believe the struggles of the women of Woodhouse are simply the result of poor personal decisions or of their individual weaknesses. I realize that their individual "weaknesses" are handicaps, because, in our current social arrangements, they ultimately contribute to subjecting these women to the direct control of others. Material and power inequities are the real odds against which they have been struggling; internalized, they produce inner conflict.

Farmer also observes that "there is much more to it than can ever meet the ethnographer's eye" (1992:255), a critical point that directs me to alternate between the readily visible and the invisible. Listening to Woodhouse women recall their experiences, sharing their memories and hopes, I sense ways larger social forces circumscribe their lives: the intersection of poverty, gender, and race, and the cultural construction of sexuality, mental illness, and homelessness. These categories form the basis of their social, cultural, and psychological "identities" and only appear to be intrinsic, natural, normal. Manipulated by the policies and practices of the various institutional settings in which they find themselves, their "identities" become useful and imperceptible tools of social control.

I am amazed that Woodhouse women somehow manage

to tenaciously hold on to life in the face of "sustained and insidious suffering" (Farmer 1996:261). In my observation, each day brings examples of kindness and love: one woman offers another helpful advice; a younger woman runs an errand for an older woman; a very sick woman, distracted by other concerns, still remembers to ask about my children. Each life story also speaks of human courage and perseverance, the limits of which are tested by the wretched conditions of our contemporary world.

Setting the Stage for Woodhouse: Political-Economic Conditions in Social Suffering

Globally, we are now in a phase of capitalism characterized by relative deindustrialization alongside expansion of a low-wage/high-wage service economy (Barak 1991; Fraser 1993; Ami 1994; I. Susser 1996). Although regional differences abound in the United States, the past twenty years have seen a general shift from traditional manufacturing to the management and production of both high-tech and low-skill services (Sassen 1991; Fraser 1993). Economic restructuring has had profound social effects, including painful consequences for many workers and the poor, and the rise of homelessness in cities (Hopper, Susser, and Conover 1986). After all, the playing field is not level, and the results of political-economic shifts are shared neither comparably nor equally. For example, as Mullings documents, high unemployment among the working class is directly related to the outmigration of jobs (1994:125). "Capital forever abandons older sectors of the economy and relocates in new and more promising industries and areas," and people are its

fallout. "Capitalism exercises an extraordinary destabiliz-
ing power in its continuous search for higher profits and
sustained capital accumulation," and human lives lie in its
wake (Schneider 1995:5, quoting Eric Wolf).

With economic restructuring has come economic dislo-
cation for those left out of the loop. In the United States,
working-class poverty increased, creating in the 1980s the
"new poverty" (Schwendinger and Schwendinger 1992).
Real wages declined, and, as greater numbers of women
found work in the service economy, the ideal of the family
wage lost its footing (Fraser 1993:13). At the same time,
spending for social programs was slashed, pushing approximately 11 million Americans into poverty by the 1980s
(Ehrenreich 1989:190).

In combination, economic restructuring and the restructuring of the welfare state set the stage for the enormous
polarization of wealth we see across the United States in
the 1990s. Housing gentrification occurs alongside housing
displacement and homelessness. As support for public services declines (from health and mental health to schools and
transportation), gross differences in the quality of private
versus public services become acute (Hopper, Susser, and
Conover 1986). These are phenomena we have been witness
to over the past two decades:

> [During the eighties] the poor had become visible again. It
> is a sad testimony to the middle-class solipsism of the eighties
> that the poor had literally to go outdoors to make their pres-
> ence known. The homeless, who captured media attention
> in the middle of the decade, are not a special breed, as they
> are sometimes presented, but only the unluckiest of the poor.
> Their own homes had been torn down, or renovated and gen-
> trified to make room for the rising corporate-administrative

stratum represented by the yuppies. Or they had been driven out by sky-rocketing real estate prices, bid up by the rich and nearly rich. The homeless stood–literally, on so many city streets–as a shocking refutation of the ongoing consumer binge: the other side of the story. (Ehrenreich 1989:240; see also Snow and Anderson 1993)

New York, perhaps the quintessential global city, has become, in Sassen's words, "[a] key location for finance and for specialized service firms [generating] the expansion of low-wage jobs," including those in the informal sector (1991:3, 10). Alongside its expansion as a leading global financial center, the city has seen a new class alignment of very high- and very low-income workers, and a labor market that remains segmented and segregated by ethnicity (Sassen 1991: 333; Stafford 1985; Hopper 1988). During these years, poverty rates have risen and income inequality has increased, and affordable housing has declined while housing gentrification has intensified. At the same time, government entitlement programs for the poor have been cut back, ethnicity has become more politicized, and poor people (and taxes) have been increasingly demonized (Weitzman 1989).

As with other cities, changes in New York's political economic landscape have also meant shifts in the sectoral location of jobs and housing, and "planned shrinkage–the denial of essential municipal services"–as responsibility for public maintenance shifted from federal to local or state governments (Harvey 1973; Wallace 1990, 1993). In one study, the authors document sorry outcomes for the poor as this shift occurs without sufficient resources at the local level to meet its new mandates (Jones, Turner, and Montbach 1992). Decentralization, coproduction, and deinstitutionalization are three interrelated policies implemented in New York City that illustrate what happens as local-level institutions, without adequate resources, are mandated to solve urban problems. Deinstitutionalization, a policy of shifting patients from psychiatric hospitals into the care of family or community support systems, offers a case in point: "patients were returned to communities and families that lacked the facilities and resources to care for them. It is now well known that many of these patients joined the ranks of the homeless" (Jones, Turner, and Montbach 1992:111; see also Baxter and Hopper 1981; Blau 1987; Dear and Wolch 1987; 1992; Burt 1992; Golden 1992; Wolch and Dear 1993). Baxter and Hopper note that by 1977, more than 126,000 mental patients were released from state hospitals to New York City (1981:31).

We also know that "[b]asic urban services are important aspects of the material resources necessary for survival, [and] their decline is threatening the ability of poor and working-class populations to maintain themselves. [But] in capitalist society there is a contradiction between human needs and the drive for profit" (Jones, Turner, and Montbach 1992:99–101). Inner-city residents don't have a fair share of the social resources necessary to maintain the "built environment" of the inner city—its houses, roads, work sites, schools, sewage systems, parks, cultural institutions (Harvey 1973; Jones, Turner, and Montbach 1992). Rayna Rapp poignantly explains the effects on human lives: ravaged by inequality, inner-city schools at once "distort children's potential [and] cannot prepare low-income youth for an economy in which they are basically redundant" (1995:187; see also Kozol 1991).

The growing income gap between rich and poor is both

an indicator and an outcome of these processes. "Income disparity in the United States is now the widest it's been since the crash of 1929," according to Zepezauer and Naiman (1996:11). Data from 1996 show that the income share of the poorest 20 percent of Americans is 3.7 percent while that of the wealthiest 5 percent of Americans is 21.4 percent (Brock 1998). Put another way, "the income of the top 1% of Americans now equals that of the bottom third (33%) of the population" (Brock 1998).

Poverty researchers Aaronson and Cameron consider the poverty rate "a rather blunt tool for understanding the actual living standards of the poor," because it fails to capture those in "extreme poverty" or those who live above the arbitrary povery-level mark of $16,485 for a family of four (1997:9; see also Collins 1996). Over the first six years of the 1990s, the U.S. poverty rate hovered around 14 percent, with the highest rates in urban and rural areas as compared to suburban areas—21.5 percent, 17.2 percent, and 10.3 percent respectively in 1993 (Aaronson and Cameron 1997:9; Henwood 1997:183).

At 26.5 percent, the poverty rate in New York City means that three out of ten citizens are poor; unemployment hovers between 9 and 10 percent (Aaronson and Cameron 1997:2; Rosenberg 1995:ii). It is also well established that New York City's labor market is highly segmented and segregated by ethnicity, with blacks and Hispanics "concentrated in lower-level jobs in peripheral industries, many of which are declining" (Stafford 1985:vi). The glaring division of resources by ethnicity and class has pushed New York's poor (the surplus) and working poor (low-wage proletariat) deeper into the "inner-city ghetto," that imaginary breeding place of problem populations. In fact, the "inner city ghettos" are the sections (neighborhoods, census tracts) of the larger city hardest hit by the dismantling of services and infrastructural supports.

While economic restructuring has generated a surplus of poor people, it is the poor who appear to be abberant (Braverman 1974; Derber 1995). Moreover, policies and programs designed to address "social problems" seem inevitably to fail. For such a highly developed and sophisticated nation as the United States, this dismal track record seems implausible, unless these practices are not failing when outcomes are matched against underlying objectives. We often assume that these objectives are to eliminate poverty, substance abuse, criminality, homelessness, and so on. If the underlying objective, however, is to contain the "surplus" in relatively controlled settings, then current policies and practices do indeed accomplish their mission: some of the surplus find unsteady and poorly paid work in the informal sector, some are warehoused in shelters and prisons, some are intoxicated by illegal drugs and legal alcohol. Lately, many are dying off in the AIDS epidemic.

The women of Woodhouse are part of this surplus—redundant in the economy, useful as an ideological tool. The "characteristics" of the women of Woodhouse—poor, homeless (have a history of homelessness), black (for the most part), mentally ill (have been diagnosed with a mental illness), prostitutes and crack addicts (some of them)—constitute that which the popular culture has handily demonized. In the popular imagination, these women make up the devil herself, to borrow from Frances Fox Piven's analytic description of poor women's role in America.[4]

The set of images behind each "characteristic" associated with Woodhouse residents works with other pervasive ideologies to further elaborate exclusion and marginalization. Powerful among these is the "cult of individualism" tied to the doctrine of private property and faith in "achievement" (Piven and Cloward 1971:47; also see Abercrombie and Turner 1982:409). Defined as "the doctrine of self-help through work," the cult of individualism has found a footing in the United States as nowhere else. The doctrine, these days considered a moral truth, helps consign the poor to the dustbins: hard work will pay off; poverty signals laziness. Independence, hard work, self-sufficiency are virtues, while poverty is "the obvious consequence of sloth and sinfulness" (Piven and Cloward 1971:46, quoting Robert H. Bremmer).[5]

For those not consigned to the dustbin, the struggle to remain welcome goes on. "Any class below the most securely wealthy [is] insecure and deeply anxious," Ehrenreich claims, speaking for most Americans. "[We are] afraid of misfortunes that might lead to a downward slide." We have learned from the cult of individualism, however, that any reversal can be overcome by inner strength and hard work. The doctrine, then, adds to our anxiety another layer of fear: "a fear of inner weakness, of growing soft, of failing to strive, of losing discipline and will" (Ehrenreich 1989:15).

From Ehrenreich's perspective, whether "looking down toward the realm of less, or up toward the realm of more, there is the fear, always, of falling" (1989:15). Something must be done with the fear to make it bearable. Sander Gilman finds a clue in the need for society to identify the "other": "We project this fear – the fear of collapse, the sense of dissolution – onto the world in order to localize it and, indeed, to domesticate it. For once we locate it, the fear of our own dissolution is removed. Then it is not we who totter on the brink of collapse, but rather the other. And it is an-other who has already shown his or her vulnerability by having collapsed" (1988:1).

The women of Woodhouse represent collapse. As formerly homeless women, their icon is the familiar "bag lady" who "does not fall within the range of what we have been taught to perceive as normal" (Gilman 1988:12). Gendered and diseased, Woodhouse women signify melancholia: as female, "especially prone to the exaggeration of emotional states;" as mentally ill, "(either) they suffer from the sin of lethargy (or) are maniacal, out of control, and running amok" (Gilman 1988:10-11).

Gilman reminds us that in the "world of representations" our own fears are banished, "isolated as surely as if we had placed [that which we fear] on a desert island. And yet in this isolation, these icons remain alive and visible to all of us, proof that we are still whole, healthy, and sane; that we are not different, diseased, or mad" (1988:271-72). Certainly, the women of Woodhouse are icons of many things we fear, not the least of which are poverty and illness. With fear, loathing, and dread, many believe that women like these—different, destitute, diseased, mad–do prove that the rest of us are whole, safe, healthy, sane. They are not us.

But they are us. We discover, after all, these are ordinary women who share our worries, our desires, our concerns. Whether they were born into poverty or have fallen into it, theirs are stories about struggles for the rudiments of subsistence and the emotional struggles they face. Of course, all struggles are not identical. Paradoxically, by means of the women's stories, the reader may come to identify with these not so different women. Still, it is true "we" are not "they" since, despite our fears, only a few among us will ever become as destitute as they are now.

Methodology and Organization of the Book

This book is based on the hundreds of pages of field notes and interviews I gathered on thirty-nine women and sixteen staff members during the course of the research. When the time came for analysis and writing, I coded the "data" on the basis of key themes that emerged from the material, including experiences with poverty, homelessness, work, the institutional setting, substance abuse, sexual violence, mental illness, AIDS, family and interpersonal relationships, sexuality, race, gender, and food. These general themes form the main portion of the book—the narrative of ethnographic description found in the following twelve chapters.

Before setting foot in Woodhouse, I prepared a 225-question guide formulated on the basis of the larger AIDS prevention research team's objectives. I was introduced to staff and residents as a researcher studying women's health issues. While keeping the larger agenda in mind, I opted for a more interactive approach to data gathering, as qualitative researchers tend to do (Agar 1996; Williams 1989; Sanjek 1990). During the course of my two-year project, I used various qualitative methodologies, primarily participant observation, informal encounters, and tape-recorded, open-ended interviews with staff and residents. I also arranged an HIV-related women's health series at the site; participants were surveyed for their opinions on the groups. By these methods, I was able to better get to know the women of Woodhouse.

A central goal in my writing this book is to share with

readers what the women are like and my experiences with them. I hoped to find a strategy for representing the results of this project that would not homogenize the women or neglect the broad social context that frames their experiences.

I began to get to know the women during the cooking group, an organized program held at Woodhouse. In the course of the research, I found the activities involved in planning and preparing a meal a lovely way to develop special ties with individual women. While that activity was a central feature of my participatory research, our conversations did not always occur in that setting, although they appear to have in the book. By using the narrative device of presenting conversations and discussions around the kitchen table, these chronicles may be called "historias," what Ruth Behar considers part "history and story, reality and fiction" (1993: 16). Although I have taken the liberty of rearranging the setting of the narratives, I have made every attempt to stay true to the words of Woodhouse women, their own descriptions of their experiences, and our conversations together. "Woodhouse" is an invented name, and I have given pseudonyms to all residents and staff I describe in this book. In most cases, the women chose their own pseudonyms for me to use.

This book is all about ambiguity and contradiction, and the story of my project can join the literature on ethical dilemmas of fieldwork. First, as Merrill Singer has persuasively argued, politics is always close at hand; therefore "scholarly distance" is an illusion (Singer 1993: 24; 1994). I pretend to no such illusion. My work as an ethnographer at a federally funded research institute attached to a major medical center, however, suggests that I am just as much a part of the problem as the solution. David Maynard situates social scientists like myself in an urban social policy industry built around the study of the urban poor, an aspect of the capital accumulation process (1995: 2; Waterston 1993:29–30; Price 1992). Like Kostas Gounis, I cannot escape being "a representative of the discipline or institution," even as my objective is to increase understanding (1995:12; see also Farmer 1992:xi). After all, my probes are not much different from those of welfare investigators toward recipients of Aid to Families with Dependent Children (AFDC), particularly those questions centered around sexual behavior and drug use (Piven and Cloward 1971:166–67). However else they may be described, my encounters with the women of Woodhouse are "power-laden between researcher and researched . . . [and] the researcher inevitably exploits her subjects' friendship for privacy-invading information" (di Leonardo 1991: 31–38; see also Crapanzano 1990:148).

Other difficult issues trouble me. I wonder if the "historias" constitute data; if not, what happens to the women and my relationship with them as they become transformed into data? My social science training has taught me to keep the "I" out of things (i.e., leave the relationship out altogether), and besides, without data what do I analyze and interpret? Also, what aspects of these women and their lives constitute data important to analyze?

Perhaps the "historias" constitute "acts of moral witness." Such acts, according to Gounis, "however honorably intended, become 'deformed and indistinguishable from voyeurism by their ultimate ineffectiveness'" (Gounis 1995:12, quoting Michael Ignatieff). Like Thomas Foster, I struggle to negotiate what he calls "the double necessity": "It is necessary both to avoid appropriating the experiences of others by claiming the right to speak as an authority about their stories and to avoid ghettoizing the experiences of others as unknowable or meaningless" (1995:70–71). These are dilemmas not yet fully solved, although I do hope that my narrative strategy of letting the women speak for themselves moves toward resolving the double necessity.

Despite my contradictory role and goals, I chose to press forward with the research and the writing of this book. When the time came for me to begin writing, I discussed some of these dilemmas with four of the women portrayed in the book: Nora Gaines, Dixie Register, Hattie McFarrell, and Susan Jones. The four women encouraged me to proceed. Later that day, Nora and I went out for a cup of coffee. I spoke incessantly about the book that now loomed over my head. Nora took my hands in hers. "The book, the book, the book, you'll write the book," she admonished, "but the really important thing is—you've come into my life and I've come into yours."

1

Home, Some Place

THESE DAYS, a walking tour of any city in the United States leads one through very high- and very low-income neighborhoods. Woodhouse, designed to provide housing and other services for the destitute in New York City, is located in the northern half of Community Board District 7, which extends from 59th to 110th Streets on the west side of Manhattan (Reiss et al. 1993).[1] In the region of the district is found the Metropolitan Opera, the American Ballet Theater, and the New York Historical Society, among other elite cultural institutions. Also in District 7 are over 100 private and public schools, day care centers, and youth programs, and handfuls of museums, playgrounds, and parks. The southern half of the district houses the more affluent (and white) residents, while poor and working-class residents of color live in the area north of 96th Street. According to the 1990 census, 20 percent of households in Manhattan's Community District 7 earn $15,000 or less per year, while more than one-fourth (26 percent) of households earn $75,000. or more. At $40,852, the median household income masks a great class divide (U.S. Bureau of the Census 1990). The women of Woodhouse are among those at the bottom of the divide.

Woodhouse looks like any other six-story brick structure along Manhattan's Upper West Side. Most likely, passersby would not notice the trim building sandwiched between others on Amsterdam Avenue. But Woodhouse is a supervised community residence that provides "formerly homeless, mentally ill women with living quarters, meals, security, structured activities and support services," according to the annual report of the not-for-profit agency that manages it. Woodhouse is one of several sites the agency operates, which include drop-in centers and transitional and permanent residences. Established about twenty years ago, this organization was in the forefront of providers serving homeless women.

The area immediately around Woodhouse is busy, and there are few vacant storefronts. Instead, small stores are filled with shopkeepers busy selling fresh fruit and vegetables, "Indian" jewelry, beauty services, discount children's clothing, groceries, pizza, deli sandwiches, and Chinese food.

When I arrive at Woodhouse on my first visit, it is around noon, and Jill, the case manager I am to meet, is out to lunch. The receptionist assures me she will be back shortly. This gives me a chance to see how things go in the dayroom, with its comfortable chairs and the TV tuned to ABC's afternoon soap opera line-up. Several women seem to be watching, but it is hard to tell if any are paying much attention. At various points when the soap opera stars begin to shout or become hysterical, people come in to take a look—Patricia, a case manager, Gus, a receptionist/guard, and some of the women hanging out at the entrance of the house smoking one cigarette after another. Today is a beautiful spring day with a lot of people outdoors and in the streets.

Residents come in and out of the lobby in a steady stream the entire time I sit waiting for Jill. There are five women in the room with me while I wait. A black woman, shoulders stooped over a pile of papers in her lap, studies a notebook of musical notation. Two women sitting hip to hip don't say a word. Two other women are over by the TV, but they don't appear to be really watching *One Life to Live*. Their names are Dixie Register and Hattie McFarrell, and we will all get to know each other better in the days to come.

Prompted by the shouts from the soap, Patricia comes running in. "Looks to me as if an incest story is about to be revealed," the social worker notes excitedly. Hattie has been staring intently at a blank wall, twirling her salt-and-pepper pigtails in a duet between her fingers. She turns to the case manager to say, "That incest story is old news," and gives all the details of the story line (Melanie is abused by her father; her stepmother is about to tell all).

I introduce myself to the two women who are sitting so silently, but neither chooses to respond. Margery Santana paces in and out of the dayroom, running stubby fingers through her fine, straggly hair. Over and over again she tells Patricia about how she has just seen the doctor and he gave her medicine for her bladder infection. Only when she begins to talk about her mother, upset that doctors had taken blood from the older woman, does Patricia abruptly cut her off: "It's good you've gotten the medicine for your infection, and I don't want to hear anything more about your mother."

Jill arrives and apologizes for having me wait. We walk to the library room, which is where the kitchen is also located. Some women come in to get started on the cooking group session and help Jill unpack the groceries. Jill explains that "cooking" is a very open group–sometimes four women come, other times fourteen women attend. The door is always open so that any woman can come in and go out as she pleases, unlike other programs that are closed to more participants once a session starts. Dixie joins in and so do Teri Jay, Nora Gaines, Margery, Susan Jones, Tinkie Deegan, a frail, silver-haired, white woman named Lillian Stokes, and Sharlea Kent, a black girl who drifts dreamily into the room without a sound. Before long, this group of ordinary women will detail to me their collapse into homelessness. I realize they share with each other the fact of that common experience, and that it has brought them together at Woodhouse.

In time I also learn that many residents consider Woodhouse their last stop and do not intend to ever go elsewhere. This is so even though the community residence is, for the most part, considered one step before "independent living," according to Victoria Leyton, Woodhouse's clinical director at the time of the research. Describing the model adopted by her agency, Victoria explained the steps toward independent living for a woman in this system: go to a city shelter and receive documentation that you are homeless; move to a transitional living center where there is a little more autonomy, although you may sleep in a bed on a floor with other people and have only a little cubicle to call your own; move to a SRO–where you have your "own room, four walls, and a door;" and move to a community residence, "a highly staffed, semi-structured living setting with an on-site food service and which provides pharmacotherapy, individual and group counseling and psychosocial rehabilitation."

I help out in the kitchen and, with Teri, wash lettuce and the other vegetables for a salad. Teri is a middle-aged

woman whose easy smile draws me toward her. I can tell
she is fastidious, with her short, ebony curls tied back tight
in a cotton kerchief and her insistence that we wear uncomfortable rubber gloves while handling the food. We chat
while we work. I ask her about her background, and she
asks me about mine.

Teri, who traces her background to "the Seminole tribe of
Indians," was born in Philadelphia but has spent most of her
life in New York–Brooklyn, Bronx, Queens, and Manhattan.
She has no family–"they all died of cancer and tuberculosis"
except her brother, who died last summer in a swimming
pool accident. Teri has lived at Woodhouse for the past year–
June will mark her one-year anniversary. She loves it at
Woodhouse and enjoys all the activities offered, especially
cooking. Teri is one of nearly fifty residents who get rooms
of their own, generally a twelve-foot by twelve-foot space
sparsely furnished with the basics: bed, dresser, closet,
chair, and night table, and one shared bathroom on each
floor.[2]

"When I was a little girl, I had a dollhouse that had a little
kitchen in it with a little stove that actually worked. I loved
the dollhouse and I would pretend cook and bake while my
mother prepared dinner."

Nora cuts us off. "Do you have your own home?" she
wants to know.

"Yes," I answer. She seems to understand not only the material divide, but the ideological divide between us. If homelessness represents collapse, "home" is its equally potent
opposite. I have home, health, strength, goodness; she has
homelessness, disease, collapse, evil.[3]

Her jet-black eyes like perfect marbles are fixed on mine.

Nora continues to stare at me, steady and sober, "Do you think this is a shelter?" "Well, no," I reply, "I understand this is a community residence."

"That's right," she asserts, "This is *my* home."

Nora throws things off with her second question. Here, Nora finds a way within the rigid dichotomy to place herself and her neighbors on the side of good. Woodhouse is home after all. I sense the fighter in her, Nora struggling against the odds.

Nora continues. "I know a lot of people think Woodhouse is a shelter, and it's not. I know what a shelter is because I've lived in a lot of them all over the city." When Nora mentions 350 Lafayette, a murmuring of yesses fills the small room. "I lived there twelve years ago," says Dixie. Tinkie once lived there too, and maybe Margery.

"I went through that system, 350 Lafayette." Nora describes what it's like.[4] "You go there at night, take a shower, you're out in the morning. They keep your bed if you show up. You don't show up at night, you don't have a bed. A lot of theft went on in there. I was in the East Side shelter, I was in the West Side shelters—it's the same type of setup. If you're in the bed at night, [you] keep that bed; if you don't come, you lose that bed, then you're out on the street.

"Sometimes, I'd get tired of the aggravation in the street and I wanted a bed, so I'd go there. So I'd go to 350, sit there all day, they'd find a shelter for me for a bed. If you lose that bed, they gonna have to find you another bed, some other shelter that's vacant. That was that type of system which a lot of people hate. A lot of people would rather sleep on a park bench all night than go through that. It was hectic. Then there's other places you could go but you couldn't lie down. You have to sleep up in chairs. I don't know why—that was the law. It got so uncomfortable where I would lay my head on the table all night, my legs would be hanging from the chair. Then when I would wake up in the morning, my whole leg would be swollen because of poor circulation. It was bad on the older people, because if you're older, the skin would break and blood would start oozing out and their legs would get full of pus. Oh, oh, I hated that position.

"So, that's why—the people who say, 'Well, why don't you go to a shelter if you're homeless?' They won't go because there's a lot of theft goes on in there, people steal from each other, a whole lot of nonsense, people get beat up and all that stuff. And the people who worked there, they were cranky as all hell, a lot of them. Cranky and mean. They didn't come in with a good attitude. It was rough for everybody."

Each woman's path to homelessness, to shelters, and finally to Woodhouse has been different, but the anguish is the same. In each of their stories, we hear how fragile having a home is. For some, having no place to live is related to mental illness. For others, the "breakdown" comes later, after suffering one too many assaults. Dixie, for example, who had lived on the street for nearly nine years, was diagnosed with bipolar disorder only after many years on the street. Others who seem to hang in the balance between emotional and material vulnerabilities are thrown over the edge by one last straw or another.[5]

The psychiatrists still can't figure out what to say about Nora. One week they say she has a borderline personality disorder; the next, she is bipolar; after that, she is narcissistic; and later, just anxious. I come to learn that at Woodhouse, there are a handful of such "borderline" cases, in which the presence of mental illness is uncertain. Because at Woodhouse mental illness is tied to residence eligibility and other bureaucratic concerns, diagnosis is critical for reasons other than the medical treatment of an illness.

It is common practice for staff to refer to Woodhouse residents as "mentally ill women." Invoking the category helps reestablish the authority of practitioners assigned to treat them. Even so, the reality of mental illness is not in question here, and most Woodhouse women do experience it. As Sander Gilman advises, it is important we not "deny the reality of the experience of [mental or physical] disease [that would] marginalize and exclude the ill from their own world" (1988:10–11). As diagnosis becomes dependent on other factors, however, the truly ill are denied the reality of their experience of the disease, and those who are not mentally ill are still subject to its stigmas.[6]

Later I also learn that Nora nearly always represents her mental state in the language of mental illness, even though it has been difficult to diagnose in her case.[7] For now, we're just getting to know each other.

"I was homeless for four and a half years, starting when I was thirty-three years old." Nora bounces to her feet to take the stage. She can't tell this story sitting down. "I went in the army in 1980, 1982. I could only do two years. I got out the army with a big resentment and anger and rage towards men 'cause I was really feeling a lot of hostility towards the army because it had a lot of discrimination towards people of color and people of sex–what do ya call it? ah, towards women. So I went back to drinkin' and druggin', my usual spot in Harlem, and I went to live with my sister.

"Now when I go up to Harlem to see my sister, my other sister up there, it bothers me to the point where I remember all the bad times I used to have. And I remember all the good times–when I first went to Harlem, we had a lot of fun drinkin' and druggin' and messing around, and bars, after-hours spots, and still abusing myself. But when we got very deep into it, it got really miserable towards the end.

"So then, now after down the line, what happened was I got tired of the whole scene and I left. I had gotten some money from the army which I saved up and they sent it to me–a couple of thousand dollars, 'cause I was good at saving what I had. During the time I was drinkin' and druggin', well, me and my sister threw that money away partying.

"I began to start to hate the scene, so I decided to go on my own. I had a little bit of money left. Go on my own. So I went and I found a room in this man's apartment. Everybody knew him. His name was Mr. Harris, but he was a little old man. So he started telling me that I couldn't–by this time, this is where I met Charlie–Mr. Harris started telling me I couldn't bring Charlie up to my room. He started telling me that if I'm staying in my–his– apartment, I should see that the dishes are clean. I said, 'Wait a minute, hold it, hold it. Not if I'm not using the dishes. I didn't come here to rent a room to be your maid, Mr. Harris. If you want a maid, you clean up your apartment, but I take care of my room. And if I use dishes in the kitchen, I clean up those dishes. I didn't come here to be your maid or your wife or nothing like that. I have Charlie, and now you want to tell me I can't bring Charlie in your–in my–home, which I pay rent here?' So that's the confusion we started gettin' into. So eventually I left, I couldn't take it.

"Then Charlie moved me over to his mother's house, which we stayed in his room. I couldn't take that either anymore. I didn't feel right. I didn't feel comfortable, and I was so unhappy because I didn't have my own. And I was sick and tired of people's stuff, you know, so I just picked up and I left.

"I left and I remember when my mother used to take us to sleep with us in Penn Station when we were little 'cause she used to move around a lot and we could not find a place to live. She had five kids at the time. So I went down to Penn Station. So I remembered that, so I went back."

The only Japanese American resident of Woodhouse, Sarah Devine, has been in New York only two years. Despite having dropped out of high school in the tenth grade due to "personal problems," Sarah had an "administrative" job in San Francisco for eleven years, earning $30,000 by 1991. Then her husband of twenty-four years died, and things started to fall apart. After she sold their home, keeping $100,000 from the sale, she invested it all in the stock market on the advice of a financial consultant. At one point, Sarah took a two-week trip to Russia with a tour group. On her way back from this trip, she stopped in New York and she stayed. As it turned out, Sarah had less money than she thought. She was broke and became homeless. For a while, she lived in a shelter on 44th Street, until a trip to the psychiatric ward at Bellevue ultimately led her to Woodhouse.

The early 1990s were tough years for Lynda Valentine, proud grandma of five-year-old Antoine. Lynda spent four years, as she puts it, "homeless." She moved from place to place, most of them shelters, until arriving finally at Woodhouse. Lynda aches for her old home. "It was Section 8 housing. I had four beautifully fixed nice rooms. I lived alone and had SSI."[8] It only took one night for everything to change. "I was attacked and beat up in my apartment," recounts Lynda with a dispassion that belies the savagery and shock of the experience "It was five or six guys." After that, she couldn't live there any longer. "I couldn't go back, she explains impassively. "They robbed me and everything, so I went from shelter to shelter."

Violence also pushed Hattie over the edge into homelessness, although she makes it very clear that a series of
circumstances rather than one horrible event accounts for
her drift toward Woodhouse. Hattie, with a knack for detail,
spreads many memories across the library table, where we
also carry on with the food preparations. While others prepare a batter, tenderize chicken breasts, and peel onions,
Hattie twists a paper napkin and talks.

Originally a farm girl from the Midwest, Hattie thought
she had found home in New York City. From 1973 until the
early 1980s, she was living comfortably in her Park Slope
brownstone, independent and working as a secretary for
years. Toward "the end," as she refers to it, Hattie had only
temporary work, which meant she had barely enough
money to pay for food, rent, and utilities. After a while, she
didn't have enough money to keep a phone in the apartment.

At a bad time for Hattie, her building's owners decided
both to renovate and to raise the rent to about $1000 a month.
There was no way Hattie could afford such a rent on her
little bit of salary. Still, she struggled along.[9]

During the renovations, many of the other tenants in the
building had moved out. The building was almost deserted.
On her way home from work one day in 1982, inside the
building two men grabbed Hattie and pulled into her apartment. They raped her for six hours. They broke her jaw, and
"there was blood everywhere." At ten o'clock that night, the
men left. Hattie feels lucky to have been found by a friend
who happened by to visit. "He walked into a blood-soaked
apartment," says Hattie.

Hattie was relieved to find that she was not pregnant and
had no diseases as a result of the rape. She waited to get a
clean bill of health from the doctors before she dared tell her

mother about the rape, a "traumatic experience," as Hattie refers to it.

"The men pulled a knife on me and threatened to slit my throat if I screamed. They kept it up for hours. They pulled my hair and wads of hair was pulled out, so later my head was covered me with bald patches. They also punched me in the stomach. For a long time I could only take in milk and juice. One week after the rape, I was in Kingsborough Hospital. I had a nervous breakdown."

Hattie couldn't bear to live in that apartment anymore, "not another day," but she went back for a month. Then she left, knowing she might have to go to a shelter. Somehow she managed to get the "proof" she needed that she was homeless. Soon she moved into a residence similar to Woodhouse. It was important to Hattie that the residence didn't allow men in the rooms or hallways. Two years after the rape, Hattie remembers going to a disco sponsored by the residence. "I stayed with a cluster of women, but then I danced with a couple of men. I even danced a couple of slow dances, and I wasn't traumatized by it."

Dixie's slide into homelessness was more gradual, not so abrupt. She had been married to "an epileptic," whose illness forced her to quit her job as a dental assistant to take care of her husband at home. As Dixie explains it, she became homeless after her husband died. She no longer received his disability checks and was not able to pay the rent.

"I went to work at Astroland in Coney Island. I cleaned toilets and made a pretty good salary. She paid me above scale and whatever I made in tips, so it was pretty good. She gave me enough rent for a hotel—a cheap hotel. The landlord was very nice to me. He would never let me pay rent on rainy days because I didn't work when it rained. But the season ended, came October and I had nothing to do and no place to go, so I lived off the Boardwalk 'til the deep winter set in.

"There I met a man who was having a hernia operation, and he said he needed a housekeeper. I took it–I was broke, I had no choice. He was very nice to me, he took me to his place of business, out to lunch, [and] he would take me out to dinner for holidays. Then he had a hair transplant, so I stayed on a little bit longer. But then it came time to leave.

"He gave me a $500 bonus when I had to leave and he sent me on my way, and it was time for me to go. It was right after that, really, that I became homeless and I hit Manhattan. And I became a prostitute and a street walker and a street sleeper."

As a postscript to her story, Dixie went back to the weeks following her husband's death. Her father-in-law traveled from his home in Havana, Cuba, to New York upon the death of his son. He urged Dixie to return to Havana with him, since she was "part of the family now." Dixie declined the invitation, explaining to her father-in-law, "I couldn't do that, I'm an *American*." Five weeks after her husband died, she was evicted from their apartment and so began her 8½ years on the streets of New York.

Diane Williams was lucky for a while; she had family to help her out during the rough times. She lived with her brother Sammy for a long time. Sammy, who is "in the military," owns a two-family house in Brooklyn. He was sent to Desert Storm, leaving his wife in the main part of the house and Diane in the basement. According to Diane, conditions in the basement were atrocious. Despite her paying rent, her brother refused to make repairs. Finally, Diane moved out because "it was terrible, the basement was flooded, water seeped into it, and my brother wouldn't let me move upstairs."

The next day she went to stay at a drop-in center for the homeless where you could stay the night, if you could sleep in a chair. Over several months, a caseworker from the center found Diane many different shelters around the boroughs. "I went all over," says Diane, "one time to a church in Brooklyn—it was nice." She finally landed in Woodhouse after telling her caseworker that she "wanted to try another place."

Teri, the pleasant smile still on her face, looks up from her handiwork on some fresh peppers. It seems that several years ago, she lived in "a Catholic residence." Ultimately, she was "kicked out" for violating curfew and spending some nights with her boyfriend. After one too many overnights, the director called Teri into her office. The conversation, as Teri recounts, went this way:

"I guess you have another place to stay, so we want you to pack your things and move there," the director told Teri.

"I don't have another place to live," Teri explained, "I was just staying the night with my boyfriend."

"Well, I guess you have another place to stay," repeated the director.

Teri had no choice. She moved into her boyfriend's apartment in Brooklyn temporarily. One day, he informed her that she could no longer stay, because his other, pregnant girlfriend was moving in. The other young woman's mother had kicked her out of the house, and Teri's boyfriend said he had no choice. That was about six years ago, and Teri says, "I haven't had sex since."

Dominique Deveroe's story is very different. Dominique found herself on the street when she aged out of a group home for youth. She became homeless "because my time was up, I was twenty-one years old." Dominique bounced from shelter to shelter in New York until she decided to head west to find her fortune. When she first went to California, she "imagined that I'd be able to go to college, get my own apartment and go on welfare." Droplets of sweat appear across her wide forehead, and Dominique laughs heartily. "I went to California thinking that I would make it out there, and I ended up on the street and I kept getting my clothes stolen."

Dominique says she was homeless and living on the street in Los Angeles for two years. She explains, "I didn't actually live on the street all the time, 'cause I lived in a women's shelter for some time."

Her voyage back to New York was courtesy of an L.A. psychiatrist and a Greyhound bus ticket. Dominique recalls the events leading up to her eviction from the state. "I was in LAX airport and taking luggage carts each for 25 cents to eat lunch and a cop said I can't do that." She caught his attention because of an unfortunate mishap on an airport escalator. It seems Dominique caught her finger on one of the luggage carts as she stood at the top of an escalator. As she tried to free her finger, the cart toppled down the escalator. That's when the officer came along to ask her what she was doing. She tried to explain, but he said she couldn't work the carts anymore. Dominique confesses, "I started calling him names like nigger and stuff, even though I'm black." Dominique tried to run away from the policeman, and she ended up in a mental facility. "They gave me an injection to calm me down," but, she insists, "I was already calm, it's just I was running away." The next day, according to Dominique, a psychiatrist asked her where she was from. She told him, and the next thing she knew, she had a bus ticket to New York.

Back in New York, Dominique spent one night "in a mansion shelter for older people" and was transferred to 350 Lafayette the next day.

Patsy Clark has been on her own since she was sixteen years old, when she left New York and moved to Atlanta,

Georgia. The Salvation Army gave her a place to stay and found her a job. She worked in a factory putting roach spray in boxes. Out of her earnings, Patsy paid the Salvation Army about ten dollars a month for rent. Patsy only lasted in Atlanta for a couple of months.

From Georgia, she found her way back to New York, where she more or less just rode the subways; she "mostly went on the trains and where the other homeless people were." Somehow she managed. "People helped me out, and sometimes I'd follow guys home and I also went to the churches."

When I ask Debra Brown how long she has been homeless, she answers, "All my life."

Sharlea Kent says she prefers not to talk about her past. "I've gone through some changes, and I don't like to talk about it."

MARGERY WALKS into the library just as the food is being served. "That Patricia's mean to me. Everyone else got their bank note except me. Why'd she pass over me?" she asks of no one in particular. The bank note, I find out later, is an allowance each woman receives from her case manager. It comes out of her Supplemental Security Income (SSI), managed by the agency.[10]

Everyone ignores her except Susan. Susan is like that. A pasty-faced, plump woman, Susan has a plain-Jane look and an extraordinary knack for friendship, loyalty, and extending a helping hand.

"May I be direct with you?" Susan asks Margery. "I think you're bothering your caseworker because you're going to her for every little thing. She's getting fed up with you and if you would quit it, she wouldn't act that way with you. You have to learn how to handle her, and you're not."

Margery quiets down a little, though not much. Susan presses her. "Am I getting through to you?" she asks.

Margery whimpers, "It's my stomach. It's bothering me from the medicine I have to take."

Before long, all the women clear out of the little library, where we have shared a very American meal of chicken wings and breasts in Shake 'n' Bake, with potatoes and onions fried in oil and a salad of iceberg lettuce, tomatoes, and green peppers.

2

Some Kind of Nobody

Norma Harris is standing outside Woodhouse, one leg bent, leaning against the wall of the building, as usual. I see her each time I come, but we've never been able to get beyond a friendly yet formal hello. I hear she may not last long at Woodhouse, because she's into crack and harasses people for money.[1]

It's up to me to initiate the greeting: "Hi Norma, how are you?" I ask, as I press the bell to be let inside the building. Norma whispers, "Fine, thank you, how are you?" so softly I can barely hear her.

I've long since given up trying to get to know her better. I know this hello is as close as we'll ever get.

Residents and visitors alike are buzzed into the building from the front desk on the main floor. I step into the vestibule, which is lined with fifty small cubbies for mail. This entranceway is large enough to hold a wooden bench where women may sit and rest, or pull off their boots in the wintertime. Past the reception counter, manned by a resident in the work program or by staff security, the first floor opens up to several common areas. These are pleasant enough, although the scent of disinfectant is an ever-present reminder of institutionalization.

42

The first floor houses case manager offices and the nurse's quarters. As clinical director, Victoria supervises the clinical staff of four case managers, the nurse, and an activities director.

Among their official duties, case managers "observe and monitor the client's behavior, noting and encouraging client progress, reinforcing positive behavior, monitoring health decompensations and arranging for interventions as appropriate," according to the agency's job description. While case managers have regularly scheduled meetings with each client, they also have frequent informal encounters with them.[2]

During her tenure, Victoria has implemented a philosophy that sets the tone for the daily workings of Woodhouse. Victoria considers Woodhouse a particularly "successful residence" compared to others around town, because "the women are able to blossom here." She explains that at other sites, residents are often forced to participate in certain structured activities, either in-house or offered at The Bridge or Fountainhouse, social service day programs on the West Side for people with mental illness. At Woodhouse, Victoria says, "There is less structure—we do not mandate their participation in programs," although various activities are available. Victoria believes this less directive philosophy "empowers the women and helps them prepare for independent living." In Victoria's words, "The looser we are, the more it works."[3]

Today at Woodhouse, I survey the dayroom to see who is hanging around. The main dayroom has dated but comfortable armchairs, a newly lacquered wooden floor, a fish tank in full operation, hanging baskets of ivy and aspidistra, and a twenty-inch color TV set. Dixie is there, magazine in hand and lost in thought. The soap is on and I still can't tell if she is paying attention to it. I excuse myself to the other women as I cross in front of the TV to get to her. Dixie, who hails from Louisiana, is the Creole daughter of a New Orleans river gambler. Now in her fifties, Dixie's gone through hell, and she often wonders if it shows. Sometimes it does, sometimes not.

"What's new?" I ask, "and what's for cooking group today?"

Dixie looks up from her magazine. The furrowed brow and pursed lips melt into a broad smile. We give each other a big hug and kiss hello, something I come to look forward to whenever I visit Woodhouse. "Not much," she drawls in an accent more Brooklyn than southern. "I'm not sure. I heard something about black-eyed peas and rice."

We make our way to the library/kitchen where we can really chat. A hall at either side of two stairways is large enough to hold a small couch, a Coca-Cola vending machine, and an enclosed public telephone booth. From here it is a short step to the library/kitchen, a multipurpose activity room in which Woodhouse hosts an array of in-house activities for its residents—the library, clothing distribution, art and quilting class, therapy sessions, and the cooking group.[4] Like a Manhattan studio apartment, the "room" has a small, square kitchenette, a bathroom, and a main room, its green walls lined with bookshelves holding hundreds of donated paperbacks. A table for eight sits in the center of the room.

As we get comfortable around the library table, which also serves as the cooking group's chopping board, food counter, and dining room table, Dixie asks, "How are the kids? How are things at home?" I tell her I took the kids to see a new movie called *Far from Home: The Adventures of Yellow Dog*, about a boy and his dog lost in the wilderness for two weeks. They survived, and the point of the movie is how this heroic teenager manages to adapt to the harsh surroundings, finding food and shelter until the rescue crews arrive.

Similarly, homeless women also struggle first for the rudiments of subsistence, whether they were born into poverty, like Nora, Patsy, and Debra, or have fallen into it, like Dixie, Hattie, and Sarah. Only, for women living on the street, vulnerability appears in various forms, and they are never thought of as heroes. Today I learn about the gendered nature of the experience and hear how some survival strategies, like prostitution, are risky endeavors both psychologically and physically.

I ask Dixie to tell me what it was like for her on the street.

"In the beginning you get woken up by the cops in Penn Station about five-thirty in the morning. You go to the bathroom and wash up and whatever clothes you have, you put on clean. You know, that was one thing I always did, my laundry, even when I was out on the street with whatever changes of clothes I had, I did [it] in the Laundromat. I went for coffee and a bagel or donut and then put on the makeup, the earrings, and the jewelry, and get all dolled up and started looking for johns. At about ten o'clock in the morning. And whatever bed sleep I got was if they would get a hotel or not. Some would get it in a doorway—as long as I got my money, I didn't care.

"I didn't make a lot of money. I would pick up maybe three or four johns at thirty-two dollars a piece—sometimes fifteen, depends on what they wanted you to do. I didn't get too kinky. I didn't go for anal sex, I didn't go too much for oral sex. If the guy was a married man and he was clean and he would have a condom, I would do oral sex, if he was generally just out for a pickup, but if it was some bum off the street that wanted a piece, I wouldn't go that route, just straight sex. Thirty-two dollars for straight sex.

"There would be about four or five a day, but that money would go—you needed to keep yourself up. You needed your makeup, you needed expensive clothes, heels, stockings. You couldn't go looking like a bum. You needed a place to shower.

"I would go to the Penta to shower, the Penta Hotel I think it was. I would go to a hotel and rent a room and do a general overhaul. I would go about every second day. I kept myself clean. I never had any kind of vaginal infection. I would get checked about every six months. I kept myself up that way.

"I always had the same amount of johns. I kept it at that amount, about five a day. I wasn't too good at it, to tell you the truth. I don't know why, I just didn't have the 'suavey.'"

This comment has us laughing and it takes a while to get back on track. I ask, "Well, how'd you feel about this?"

"Numb, just numb. I needed the money—that's all I did it for and I was just numb, I didn't feel anything.

"I was in the Penn Station area for many years, about five years. I met other prostitutes and developed friendships. I never got arrested, never had a run-in with the police. I don't know how I managed that. I was very lucky, very lucky, I was never arrested. I guess because I wasn't conspicuous. I also wasn't out there going for every john, you know, I was discreet. Sit next to somebody in Penn Station. And I only worked days.

"At night I slept, mostly, because it was tiring. And that's when most of the action is, at night. I'd pick up guys going to work, you know, they'd want a little something on the side before they went to work. I did a little prostituting in Coney Island also, I went back there.

"I went to Coney Island to see what was doing. My job

[cleaning toilets] was no longer available. I would have taken it up again, but they closed the bathrooms down. There was no work for me, and so I did some pickups there, some prostituting there, but not a lot. About every third day or so I would pick up a john. It was summertime, so it was easy to live off the Boardwalk.

"I collected cans, and I made myself a good fortune. As a matter of fact, I made myself about $125 a day collecting cans off the Boardwalk in Coney Island. Made myself that much money. They have a Pathmark there that has a place where they accept the cans, so you don't have to go to the supermarket and wait for the register. They just collect cans and bottles. It's like a regular business. You go in, you give them your cans and bottles–it's all done almost like a com-puter–they give you a receipt, you take that receipt, and you get your money. It was very organized. But then it closes up like everything else out in Coney Island, closes up by October.

"I lived from hand to mouth. I really didn't overexert my-self, I didn't want to get in trouble with the cops. I didn't want to overdo the sex thing. I just needed money to sleep and eat and get maybe some rags and that's all, that's just what I did. I wasn't gonna make a fortune to buy a house or anything. I knew no matter how much I would have gone for, how much more was I gonna make that was gonna make a difference?

"Then I had had it. I had about fifty-two dollars on me–no, about forty-six dollars. And I stopped two cops and I asked, 'Is there a shelter around here?' And they said, 'Yes, there is.' So they sent me to the Dwelling Place. It's on Ninth Avenue, between Ninth and Tenth Avenue and Forty-second Street. I lived there for about eight months. I cleaned my-self up.

"It was very nice, but you had to be out by eleven o'clock

and couldn't come back until five-thirty in the evening. So all they gave you was breakfast, dinner, and a bed and shower. They don't—they didn't—house. They just—it was just a place to sleep. They didn't house. It was immaculate.

"When I first went there, I told them my story and she said, 'My goodness, you really have had it.' She said, 'We've got a bed for you. We don't appreciate your doing any of that.' And I said, 'I wouldn't be here if I wasn't, I'm tired.'

"I left there after eight months to go to the Olivieri Center. It was nice except you had to sleep on chairs. And they said, 'Why don't you get started with social services?' I really didn't feel like sitting in any welfare office, and I really didn't know what I was going to do about it. But they said at the center that they would do that for you, all the social services are taken care of over there—you don't have to go to anybody's office. They deal right from the center.

"I didn't know anything about the system. My husband was on SSI. I was totally unfamiliar with it. All I knew was that he got a check because he was disabled and that we cashed it every month. That's all I knew. I knew nothing about SSI. I knew nothing about welfare whatsoever, how to get on it. My family, we never were on any kind of social services. We were *working* class."

"Where was your family?" I ask.

"All dead, all dead."

Nora chose the Port Authority Bus Terminal over Penn Station. "Homeless people," explains Nora, "switch from Penn Station to Forty-second Street, Grand Central, to the Port. That's how we did it. Those are the main stations where we knew we possibly could go to the bathroom, we could go get water, we could go get soap, we could go wash up, stuff like that.

"At first, I found it so peaceful, just to get away from Harlem and all the nonsense. I thought I could handle it, but eventually it got harder and harder and harder for me. It took about seven, eight months, then it started to get weary. I started to gettin' very weary, hopeless. I started to feel hopeless. I started to feel like I was just nobody, you know, your self-image and your self-esteem goes down when you're homeless and stuff. Life doesn't mean—your life doesn't mean anything, doesn't haven't no meaning whatsoever, you know, and it was very hard, it was horrible.

"A typical day was you get up in the morning, if I had the chance to sleep at night. Get up in the morning and go in the ladies' bathroom and wash up the best I could. Then you find places where they gives meals. So I would go there. A lot of places, The Upper Room across the street from Port Authority was one place, they had this church across the street from Penn Station—I forgot the name of it, but it's famous—still gives a lot of, deals with the homeless a lot to this day, go over there, get sandwiches.

"People would tell me—you know, another homeless person would tell another homeless person, 'You know something, you can go here.' I started to falling in line with what they were doing, and I started to get it. But then, you know, feelings, you're eating and stuff like that, but then you run into people who don't smell good and you're mixed up with them and your clothes are dirty and then you really start to really feel hopeless, you really start to feel, 'This is it, man, this is it for you, you're gonna die,' you know, that's it.

"After that I walk around, I walk around. Maybe I go to the library. I started going to the library on Fifth Avenue to kill some time. They had a park over there, Bryant Park, across the street. I used to go in there and lay on the grass and sleep. When you go in the park, nobody would bother you. There'd be people coming out of work and go lay on the grass, so how do they know I'm homeless."

WHEN NORA says this, I think she has absorbed well the cultural message that she is among those *not entitled to use public space.* It is not difficult to get the cultural message when police intermittently enforce it by shooing away "loiterers." But the public domain *does* include Nora. Aren't these spaces for use by all our citizens? Even out-of-town visitors are welcomed into them. Or is it Nora's "inability to consume," as opposed to residents and tourists with dollars to spend, that signals her exclusion from public space?

As Nora speaks, I think about a study on homelessness I've been reading. "The overriding feature [of homelessness]," say authors Wolch and Rowe, "is a relative erosion of time-space continuity, or time-space discontinuity." Describing a variety of forces buffeting homeless people, the authors consider this the most critical: "the loss of spatially fixed stations in the daily path . . . pivotal points of return in the round of routine activities [that] accumulate to form an individual's life path, or time-space biography" (1992:117, 116). This interpretation accords with Nora's poignant description of her life on the street.

"You're like this person with a backpack who's on a California somewhere, on a journey or somethin', or on a journey, you know, a journey, like that. Then, still in the midst of this, it just seems so hard because you're, you know, it's not like, I don't know, I can't explain it. You have to be homeless to really know what the mess people go through—'cause people who are not homeless, and people who are, it's not like how I'm talking.

"You're going nowhere. It's like you don't know what's up, what's going to be up next.

"At least when you have a home, you know, I'm a go out, gotcha key, put your key in the door, and I'm going, and I'm

going to do this and I'm going to do that, and I'm comin'
back. I'm gonna fix dinner, I'm gonna get the kids ready,
and maybe I'm gonna take a shower and everything is set.

"When you're homeless, nothing is set."

LISTENING TO Nora describe her experiences, I am also
reminded of prisoners of war describing theirs. I look up
Viktor Frankl's *Man's Search for Meaning,* with its classic de-
piction of imprisonment during the Holocaust in which we
learn "what a human being does when he suddenly realizes
he has 'nothing to lose except his so ridiculously naked life'"
(Allport in Frankl 1959:9, 79). Nora's words resonate in this
passage by Frankl on strategies devised by prisoners struggling to "preserve the remnants of one's life":

> The prisoner . . . escaped into the past. When given free
> rein, his imagination played with past events, often not im-
> portant ones, but minor happenings and trifling things. His
> nostalgic memory glorified them and they assumed a strange
> character. Their world and their existence seemed very dis-
> tant and the spirit reached out for them longingly: In my mind
> I took bus rides, unlocked the front door of my apartment,
> answered my telephone, switched on the electric lights. Our
> thoughts often centered on such details, and these memories
> could move one to tears. (1959:50)

Of course, that Nora is no such prisoner renders her
suffering all the more invisible. Nora is "free" to walk the
streets of Manhattan, find a little place in the Port Authority
to lay down her head, and even take a stroll through a city
park. Her existence did become "provisional in the sense
[she] could not live for the future or aim for a goal" (Frankl
1959:79). But there is no war to explain her state; must be it
ravages inside herself.

Nora goes on. "The only thing that kept me with a little hope was the churches. Because I knew that I could always go to the church. But even they, with the churches, you get so depressed, you get so low, that you don't start not even wanting to go there. So then when you get like that, you start not even wanting to take care of yourself. When you don't want to care of yourself, you want to die.

"You're afraid, you're afraid, you're afraid, you're afraid of–ah, you're afraid of, you're afraid, you have a lot of fear. So a lot of homeless people keep to themselves. They're disorientated. Their mental illness sets in, because you have depression and paranoia.

"And so then it got worse. My head got worse and I felt very, very low, depression.

"So then I noticed that people were drinking. I noticed everyone was drinking beer while they were homeless. So, maybe that's it, maybe I'll have some beer. Really what I think I was looking for was for comfort inside, to ease the pain that I was in.

"I had stopped drinkin' or druggin' 'cause I thought I should have my faculties while I was doing this. But the way I did it, it didn't work out like that. I would have loved to go through homelessness without drinkin' and druggin' because I would think it would be very, very interesting. I think I would have learned a hell of a lot more, without the drinkin' and druggin'. Four and a half years of being homeless is a lot of stuff to learn and to know, but I was drinkin' and druggin', so I lost a lot of stuff too that could have been very valuable.

"Sometimes you lay down and the minute you lay down the police were bothering you. You find a little cozy spot somewhere, get you some cardboard, lay it out, put your backpack and stuff up under you head, and that's it. Then also when you're a woman, you have men hitting on you and have to watch yourself–women have to be very careful because they can be easily raped. At one point I was, down the line.[5]

Dixie was too. Even so, she thinks it's harder for home-less men to manage than for women, because "women can always get someone to give them something, people feel sor-rier for women." She adds, "But it's hard for women because they have to worry about things like getting raped."

Dixie liked to go out late at night and just walk around, smoke her Kents, and get a cup of coffee. She'd always find someplace open and never had trouble. The streets were always quiet. One night she took a walk over by the New York Public Library on Forty-second Street. It was about two-thirty in the morning. She decided to sit on the steps of the library. This guy was there too. Dixie didn't pay much attention to him, but he said, "Good evening, ma'am," and she answered, "Good evening."

She really just wanted to sit and smoke a cigarette by her-self, but the guy started to talk to her. He moved closer to her. When he got very near, he grabbed Dixie's arm. Before she knew it, he was on top of her, raping her, hurting her.

"It didn't last very long," says Dixie, "but since the guy was big, he hurt me." While it was happening, she told her-self to think of him as just another john, just another trick. "There really was no difference," she says, "except here he could have killed me." He never did ejaculate, and finally he just ran away. Dixie says, "I should have thanked him for not killing me."

Dixie went back to her room and took a bath. She was angry, but not afraid. "I always thought I'd be scared, but I wasn't scared, just so angry." After that, Dixie never again ventured out late at night.

"Did you report it to the police?" I ask.

"What was I going to say to the police?" answers Dixie,

sounding surprised by my question. "That I was out there at two-thirty in the morning with short shorts on?"

"I think the guy just wanted a piece," she continues. "I just don't understand why he didn't just ask me, instead of just taking me as if I was nothing."

Nora did go to the police. "One night I went upstairs in one of the exits in the Port with a young fella who I met on Ninth Avenue. He said, 'Well come on, you're sleepy? I'm gonna sleep too. I'll get some sleep and you'll get sleep. This way we don't have no problems, nobody will bother you, nobody will bother me.'

"I was so tired, I wasn't thinking that this guy was going to rape me. I was just out of it, I was tired, and I had been drinking. So we goes, I lie down, we fell asleep. And I was into this big sleep. All of a sudden I woke up to–I felt, when I was asleep–my face moving like this and like that. I open my eyes, the guy was punching me. He was punching me in the face. And I woke up and he just kept hitting me in the face, punching me in the face. So then he told me. I started fighting him, and I said, 'What the hell you hitting me for?' So I started fighting him back, so he started fighting me back.

"Then he says, 'Take 'em off.' Like that, so I knew what he meant–take off my pants.

"I did everything, I did what he told me.

"All he wanted to do was have sex. So after he finished having sex, having intercourse, he said, 'Put back on your pants,' so I put back on my pants, and I said, 'Let me ask you something.' I said, 'If that's what you wanted, and you hit me and shit like this,' and my eye was sitting out swollen, it was puffy. He gave me a cigarette. I took the cigarette, and I said, 'Let me tell you something, man,' I said, 'All you had to do was ask me, you didn't have to hit me while I was sleeping.' You know, like that. So he didn't say nothin'. He gave me a cigarette, smoked a cigarette.

"I told him, I said, and he's getting ready to leave, so I said, 'I'm gonna tell you something. I'm gonna tell you something, and I want you to look me right in my face.' I said, 'I want to tell you something.' I said, 'This ain't finished, not by a long shot.' I said, 'If I ever see you again, I'm gonna have your ass arrested, I mean that.' He didn't say nothin' to me, just left. We left it like that.

"What I did was go across the street to the Dwelling Place. We used to go over there. The nuns, they fed us dinner, give us showers. So I went over there and my eye now is blackening here and it's getting more puffier. About a day after, I start crying, I start to realize what had happened to me. A nun came up to me and said, 'Nora, what happened?'

"I said, 'I was raped and I was beat up in the Port.'

"She says, 'Did you tell anyone?'

"I said, 'I didn't tell a soul.'

"She says, 'You have to, you must tell someone. I want you to get up now and go across the street, and you tell the Port Authority police and file a report.'

"I went over and filed a report. They took my report, that's about it. That's all they could do. The Port Authority police were not very kind to homeless people. Then a police took me to Bellevue Hospital, where I went to the rape crisis.

"At Bellevue, they asked me a lot of questions. And I still felt extremely bad. They told me it was not my fault, but I thought it was. I had no business going with this guy to sleep, thinking that he wasn't gonna bother me. So I beat up myself about that. So they says, 'Well, Nora, you did all the right things. We checked you, we don't think you have any diseases or anything like that.' Thank God.

"A couple of months down the road and I goes back. One day, I was walking on the lower level, my backpack on my back. I remember I was clean that day. I was into my sobriety again, trying to stay clean.

"I walk past the men's bathroom. Here's this guy, standing up in the mirror, shaving. I spots him. I remember the cop told me, he says, 'If you see him again, you are to dial this number with the phone, one of the phones in the Port.' So I see him. So I spotted him. Then I picked up the phone. I dialed. I said, 'My name is Nora Gaines. I filed a report about a rape a couple of months ago with a Detective So-and-so-and-so, and he told me to ring this number if I spotted this person again. This person is now here.' The detective says, 'Okay, where he is? Where are you?' I said, 'I'm on the lower level, on the men's bathroom, and he's standing in the bathroom shaving.' And he says, 'Okay, stand there outside the men's bathroom, we'll be right there.'

"No sooner I put up the thing, all these cops, all the Port Authority police came zoomin' down, 'cause they don't play. Port Authority police do not play, they don't play. It made me feel very good about the Port Authority police for that. That incident right there made me feel really good. I mean they zoomed down there, they rushed in the men's bathroom, they grabbed him, and they turned him around to me and they said, 'Is this him?' I said, 'Yeah. I told you I was gonna get your ass, I told you I was gonna get you.' They put him in cuffs, and he was saying, 'Ah, man, what is this?' and stuff like, you know how they do. They put him in cuffs. They took him.

"Everybody was looking at us and everything. Oh man, holy scot!

"We never went to court. I don't know why. It just never went to court. They didn't follow it through, something happened. I don't know what happened, bureaucracy or whatever. I don't know what happened. At least I was attempting to take the proper steps, and I was proud of myself for doing that.

"I had my moment of telling him, 'cause I remember I

told him, I says, 'This isn't finished.' I told him that. I told him, 'This is not finished.' I said, 'I don't let nobody do nothing to me and get away with it.'"

IN HER BOOK on the "unequal homeless," Joanne Passaro writes, "Each of us may choose, at different times and in different contexts, from among the performative dances of gender available and apprehensible to us, but dance we must" (1996:11). I see the gender dance being performed in both women's stories: the role it plays in choice of subsistence strategies (cleaning toilets, caring for people, prostitution) and in what happens to women on the street, from sexual assault to small kindnesses bestowed on "pitiful" women. After all, under certain economic conditions, gender and conformity to expected roles and duties cannot be divorced from their role in subsistence, even if their appearance cannot be fully explained by their strategic role in survival.

And these two stories of life on the street are also chronicles of strength and fighting back. Both women managed to find ways to keep clean, fed, clothed. Dixie turned the minimum number of tricks necessary for her own maintenance and was consistent in seeking preventive medical care. For Dixie, prostitution was a harrowing way to earn a living. She experienced rape as "just another trick," seeing a difference only in degree of potential violence. She walked away from the experience, feeling ambiguous about her dignity. With deference, she remarks, "I should have thanked him for not killing me"; with composure, Dixie wonders why "he took me as if I was nothing."

Nora also knows she is something, somebody, even if most of the signs around her suggest otherwise. As a street person living in the Port Authority, Nora believes the rape she experienced was her own fault, a sentiment shared by many women who have been sexually assaulted. With a little help from kind strangers, Nora found a way to stand up to the rapist. By having him arrested, Nora made good on her promise not to "let nobody do nothing to me and get away with it."

Like Dixie, Nora is ambivalent, see-sawing between self-disgust and righteous indignation. For as long as she can remember, this is how it has been. Early on, Nora learned to swallow many indignities, along the way accepting "fictions as realities about herself," as Gilman describes the psychological process (1988:3–4). But Nora wouldn't be completely tamed; she protests in anger. Of course, when Nora displays her anger in controlled settings, it becomes another "thing" in *her* to be broken.

3

Drinkin' and Druggin'

NORA GAINES is forty-four years old, a petite, wiry black woman prone to "rages" that always seem to get her into trouble. Her days at Woodhouse may, in fact, be numbered, because her violent outbursts frighten residents and staff alike. One of these outbursts nearly led to the elimination of the cooking group. The directors were concerned that, what with the knives and all, someone might get hurt.

The incident served as a reminder of Nora's vulnerability to the power others have to make decisions about her life. Then again, the housing system for the homeless serves as a constant reminder of poor people's vulnerability to dictates and schedules devised by those with the authority to enact them.

The women are also well aware that residences like Woodhouse are in scarce supply, and that not just anyone qualifies. To be eligible, women must undergo a kind of rite of passage, from certification of homelessness to referral by a city shelter, drop-in center, or another residence. The social workers and case managers who handle their cases, act as advocates, helping women enter the system, stay in it, or move out. Such advocates can also become direct adversaries, however, given their role in deciding a woman's fate, such as eviction from the residence.

Nora and I are growing close. Even though our lives have been so different, we share something deeper, almost spiritual. She says, "You have anger, but I have rage." I agree and show her this quotation from Audre Lorde: "My anger has meant pain to me but it has also meant survival, and before I give it up I'm going to be sure that there is something at least as powerful to replace it on the road to clarity" (1984: 132). Neither of us has quite figured out what that something might be. Nora–sharp, smart, and filled with self-loathing– has insight, and a wonderful sense of humor and drama. She also perceives herself as having two sides–the good and the bad. When she is good, she is very, very good, and when she is bad, she is doing crack.

Nora is also in charge of planting the Woodhouse garden in the small patio in back. This year there is no money in the budget for flowers, so I pick up a flat of annuals on my way to Woodhouse. Together we plant the white and lavender impatiens while Nora talks about the time years ago she had a "nervous breakdown."

"I fell into a deep depression. I had to go to Harlem Hospital and they told me I was about to have a nervous breakdown. They put me on Valiums and I stayed in my house for three months and I slept for three months.

"My sister would come into the room and say, 'Nora, please get out of bed. You're scaring me, you haven't come outside in I don't know how many months.' After that, I finally got enough courage to throw out the pills–but the pills actually made me commit suicide–I picked up a knife at myself–but I didn't do it, I threw it down, but I was in a lot of pain. I wasn't going to see nobody, wasn't talking to nobody. Then one day I decided to get up.

"I finally got up enough courage one day. I decided to go outside. I opened the door, peeked my head outside. It was sunny and everything like that—scared the shit out of me. I went back inside and went to bed, and I was paranoid by this time. I was just really paranoid about outside. So gradually, my sister would come in and say, 'Nora, Nora, come on, I'll take you, come on and go to the store with me. Keep your pajamas on.' That's how she did it, she kept my pajamas on me and we would go to the store together, across the street.

"She got me out, little by little.

"Finally before you knew it, I was out.

"I was out, and I went back to the famous old bar, the Cafe Lounge. I sat there and listened. 'We heard that you were sick, Nora. What happened, bah, bah.' I said, 'It's just I had a nervous breakdown, bah, bah, so I had to stay in the house, stuff like that.' 'Are you feeling all right now?' Says, 'Oh yeah, I'm great.'

"So then here comes a guy, Charlie, there comes the bar scene again, here comes the coke, here comes the alcohol again and again and again.

"So Charlie steps into the picture. Charlie is little, like me. I liked him, he liked me. He was an alcoholic, I didn't know—he drank worse than I did. But we liked each other, he was cute. I liked him, he was cute, that motherfucker. So I get back in a destructive relationship again. That led us into guns, at this after-hours spot we were working for, and I started toting a .22, he started toting a .38.[1]

"I was working with Charlie. See, Charlie did the technical stuff, the liquor. He made sure all the liquor was there in the club by a certain time. He also kept track of the receipts, and stuff like that.

"And I was his woman, so I was always by his side.

"One person was selling guns, so we let him in. He took us to the back office and we sat down and laid out all these guns. He says, 'Which ones do you want?' So Charlie picked one. I said, 'I want a gun too. If you get a gun, I take a gun too,' you know, like that.

"He loved me. Charlie adored me. He said, 'Give Nora a gun. Pick one.'

"And I felt very powerful with a gun. With them I could slip 'em in my socks or back of my pants or in my purse. By that time my hair was longer, and I wore lipstick, makeup and heels and dresses and pants suits and my minks and my rings and stuff like that.

"I guess I didn't know my true identity at that time. I was just going with the flow. In Harlem, all the women who go with big-shot guys were dressing in heels, talk smart, outside of their lip. Wore diamonds, wore diamond name rings and smoked.

"So maybe at that time I wasn't really playing the true me. Not to say I liked that life, I've come to hate it, but that's what I was doing. We had good times together, but we also had bad together.

"He wasn't very abusive towards me. He loved me. Charlie loved me. He was a little like me, and I liked that. He was cute, I liked that. And we looked very good together, I liked that. He was like a little kid, and I liked that. So I held out and I stayed with him. And I knew at times he wasn't about hitting, but I also knew that I could fight him 'cause he was little, like me, and I liked that.

"So then I decide to go into the army–one day I was in a bar–'cause by this time I'm tired. I'm tired of sitting on a stool, tired of moving from bar to bar to bar, frustrated. I met a recruiter in a bar I was in. I was in this bar on St. Nicholas Avenue. In the daytime. I decided to go into the bar, and go get a twenty of coke, sniffing coke. I go into the bar and sit and have a drink. I was so frustrated and so mad at myself because I said I'm so sick of the life, that's all we do.

"I go back and forth in the bathroom and take a sniff. I came back out of the bathroom and there was this guy in a green uniform sitting up at the bar. So I watch TV, 'Be all that you can be,' and I used to be curious about this when I be watching the TV, about all the places they went.[2]

"I see him in a uniform. I walked up to him and said, 'Excuse me, sir, but are you a recruiter?'

"And he said, 'Yes I am.' His name is Sergeant Brown, I'll never forget him. He said, 'Yes I am. Are you interested in the army?'

"I said, 'Sir, is there any way you can get me the hell out of here?' I told him just like that. I said, 'You think I can be in the army too?' Said, 'Please tell me I can go into the army.'

"He says, 'How old are you?'

"I told him something, late twenties, early thirties, so there's a long period of drinking and drugging there.

"He says, 'Here's what you do. You qualify—you're not too young or too old. So why don't I give you my card.' He turns to the barmaid and says, 'Give her a drink.'

"I taste the drink, and I'm not paying the drink any mind 'cause I'm thinking about 'Be all that you can be' and flying across the sky, different places.

"I go down to the office, took some tests. I'm so excited because this is the beginning of a new life for me. New, and it was, in its own way.

"I passed. A couple of weeks down the line he said, 'Congratulations Miss Gaines, you are now, we accept you in the army.' Oh man, I was so happy.

"And here goes the big bump. I goes uptown. I'm gonna break the news to *everybody*.

"So I go uptown and I break the news to Charlie. Charlie was in the army. *'What? What'd you say?'*

"I said, 'I'm in the army. I leave in another month.'

"He blew his stack.

"I called my mother, somehow I got hold of my mother. My mother said she thought it was great because I would have a lot of opportunities and everything. She thought it was great. My father said no because the army is for the men. My father always thought that I was queer anyway. One time I had my hair, my hair was short, he called me a freak. He called me a freak. So that hurt me too. Until now I'm self-conscious with men when I have short hair. So half of my family agrees, half disagrees.

"Well, nevertheless, I said in my head, 'Fuck you all, 'cause guess what? I'm going.'

"I reported back to Sergeant Brown who told me, 'You are to report to Brooklyn, Ft. Hamilton, on such and such a date.'

"All this time Charlie is trying to really talk me out of it. He's trying to show me what drill sergeants do to you, what they say to you, giving me all this stuff they do. He's taking me to the park and showing me how they drill you.

"I'm sittin' up there listening, 'Yeah, Charlie? They do that too?' I mean he really drilled me. And guess what? I got on the plane nevertheless.

"He was mad, he was *mad* when I got on that plane.

"I was immediately transported to Fort Jackson, South Carolina, for basic training. The basic training, it was even worse than what Charlie said. But I'm a survivor. And I'm a fighter.

"Here I am with a bunch of guys. And you know my background. I'm already full of anger, I'm already full of rage, I'm already full of bitterness. And here I am. Here I placed myself into a whole community of men. Now, if I didn't give them a run for their money, they gave me one. You have two ways of looking at it. They got what they wanted, but I gave them a particular hell.

"After I did my field unit order in Texas, I got orders to move from Texas to Frankfurt, Germany. Frankfurt, Germany, I stayed there for only a month. But nevertheless, I had never thought I would set my foot, *my* foot on Germany's soil. I never to this day ever thought or dreamed that I'd set *my* foot on Texas soil, you know.

"The platoon was transferred back to Massachusetts, Fort Devons. And there is when I start to break down, I started to get worse, my violence started to come out more, my rage started to come out more. I busted in the colonel's offices without permission with my M-16.

"I seen a lot of stuff, I seen a lot of racism in the army, I seen a lot of sexism 'cause I was a woman. That angered me more. I would always get dirty detail and I didn't like that. I thought people were out to get me.

"They wouldn't encourage me. I put in papers to go into officer's school, and they would not encourage me to do it. Another person who was white would put a paper in, and the minute I turned around, he was gone. And people in our platoon would say, 'Yeah, they let him go to officer's school, John.' And I would hear them, and that hurt me a lot, you know. I started to feel very angry at the United States Army.

"I started acting out. Okay, now, they took the M-16 away from me. They decided to send me to a psychiatrist. The psychiatrist wanted to know why I was angry and started to talk to me about bah, bah, bah, bah. He told me that what I should do is go out every time I get angry and hit a tree.

"Take a stick and hit a tree. So I said, 'I'm not gonna hit no tree because a tree didn't do anything to me.'"

NORA KNOWS the army psychiatrist is ridiculous when he suggests she hit a tree to vent her anger. Something outside her self has wounded her, and it is not the tree. Someplace inside she knows it's not all about some evil within *her*.

"My sergeant came to me and says, 'Nora, we have suggested to First Sergeant Garfield that you're a good soldier, but you have a lot of aggressiveness in you that's in the wrong direction and we need to take the proper action. We don't want you to go to prison. We think that it is best that you leave the army—we are going to give you an honorable discharge so you don't have to worry about that.'

"Then I got even more angry because again I started thinking that they were plotting against me. They didn't want me to be anybody. I went in there to be a lifer, and they didn't want me to be anyone, anybody. That's what I felt.

"I walked away from the army very angry and very resentful, and I went *back* to drinkin' and druggin' in Harlem."

It was pouring rain, a miserable day. Nora and I go to the local five-and-dime because she wants to buy her case manager, Jeanne, a package of mints. "I can't buy her something too sweet 'cause, you know, white people don't eat like that," she informs me. While we are waiting on line for the register, I notice a display of packaged condoms selling for about ten dollars a box. I say, "Nora, check this out." She takes one look at the price and at the top of her voice shrieks, "That's to put on a *thing* that's like *gold!* I don't know any like *that!* So much money just for a rubber!"

As we walk back to Woodhouse, I keep pulling Nora back off the street as we get ready to cross it. She never seems to look where she's going. "God is watching over me," she explains, "I have a guardian angel. St. Michael is a guardian angel and he's my guardian angel."

Nora steps off the curb just as a city bus makes its way around the corner. I grab her again. "Maybe you *do* have a guardian angel," I marvel.

Another time, we are at the cooking group table, chopping and chewing on fresh garlic. Nora looks at me. "If I have AIDS will you stay with me until I die?"

Nora often worries about becoming HIV positive. She feels lucky to have escaped so far, considering her years of sex, drugs, and homelessness along Forty-second Street and in the Port Authority. She knows a lot about how she can avoid or contract AIDS and has been tested for HIV several times. In her diary, Nora writes:

> I love all people. But I just don't like most people.
> I have learned to not take myself too seriously and no one else because we are sick people.
> I am grateful because there are people here at Woodhouse who are worst off then me (God help them). I am sick too so I will rest and relax and help with the more helpless people here and out there in the world.
> I don't trust nothing crack says to me now. No matter how good it sounds, it lies.
> Crack is a deceiver and a liar to me, alcohol and sex too.
> Save me from any diseases or help me to live with it a day at a time in a positive way.
> I may be HIV positive.

Sometimes Nora says she uses a condom during sex. She wants an HIV test because "I don't trust condoms." Sometimes Nora says she doesn't use condoms. She might have just spent four nights sleeping in the park and having "unprotected sex" with "five, six, seven different men."

Recently, Nora was on the run for about three weeks. And sex and safety? Again, I'm grilling.

"Why do you want to know so much about it?" she snaps. "Tell *me* about your weekend with your husband. Did *you* have a lot of sex?"

"I will tell you this," she says, turning the tables back to our usual, inequitable dynamic where I ask the questions and she gives the answers. "I've had sex in the most romantic, exciting, dangerous places in New York City–the subway tunnel, and under bushes in the park," she murmurs, looking to see how this bit of information touches my middle-class sensibilities.

"I gotta go see Jeanne right now, Nora suddenly announces one day. "She wants me to go to a live-in treatment place."

"What's going on?" my inquiry begins.

"I can't seem to stay straight by myself." Nora tries hard to be nonchalant, maybe hoping I will stop asking her so many questions.

"Why don't you want to tell me?" I push a little.

Nora shrugs. "I keep relapsing, that's all."

"What's the matter, do you think I won't like you?" I challenge her angrily. "I already know you do drugs, and I still like you, so what about that?"

Nora holds me tightly to her.

Just the other night, she was tempted to go on the street again, "for the excitement." This time, Nora "prayed to God for ten minutes and it went away. I was already in bed when the urge came over me. At first I was thinking about how exciting it would be to go up and down the street, looking to score. Then I reminded myself it's all a big lie. Crack's just like a man who betrayed you–you can't ever believe him again. I try to remember you can't ever trust crack, it'll betray you again."

We are talking about what it's like for her, getting high on crack. Some days, the urge to do crack is not so great, and Nora can resist. Some days, the urge is so great, Nora can't help but go out and prowl the street, only to be hit with overwhelming remorse later.

"I want the feeling the drug gives me." Nora jumps out of

her seat, puts her whole body into the description of a crack high. I'd like to understand its appeal. "I feel the toke," she coos, lingering on the thought. "How it feels when it goes down my throat, all through my chest. It's pure pleasure, peace, contentment."

"Then that other side says, 'Don't do it, it's bad, it's evil, oh please God, give me the strength to resist this, what are you doing to yourself?' Admonishing herself, Nora draws on dominant representations of the "dope fiend addict": "You're weak, evil, you're an addict, sick," she tells herself. With each relapse, self-reproach becomes new evidence for Nora of her own "unworthiness."

Nora says that before a relapse the first side isn't saying anything, "It's just the feeling that I have. Before you know it, my shoes are on my feet—" Nora stops in midsentence and makes herself the actor. "Before I know it, I'm putting on my shoes and walking out the door."

It's only later that self-loathing, anxiety, paranoia set in. These feelings last a long time—days, weeks. Self-loathing, anxiety, paranoia, rage, loneliness, boredom, longing, and Nora is out the door again.

THIS TIME, I am in the dayroom with Teri, Dixie, Sol Revilla, and Lynda Valentine. Nora pokes her head in to say hello and quickly disappears. I go after her. She says everything is fine, but she seems annoyed, irritated. I pursue it. "What's the matter?" I ask, "what's bothering you?" Nora shrugs. I ask if she has received the results of her HIV test. She hasn't, she's afraid to go, to find out. We pause, an unusual quiet when we are together.

Nora picks up the conversation again. "I've been obsessing over it. I'm sure the results are going to be bad. I just don't want to know. I don't want to find out my life is over."

"Okay," I say in my best take-charge persona, "let's go there now, all right?"

"What?"

"C'mon, I'll go with you—let's go over there now, okay?"

Nora smiles a little smile and whispers okay. We walk down the street to the city health office just around the corner. Almost immediately, Nora seems more relaxed. She talks about obsessing over the results and how it had gotten the better of her. On Tuesday, she had an all-nighter in the park, smoking crack. Nora calls it "a relapse" and blames it on her "mood." "My mood got so down," she says.

Now she's looking up and thinking about taking karate lessons at a place on Broadway. "I'm sure Jeanne will say I can't." Nora curls her lip girlishly, feeling sorry for herself.

I DON'T THINK this is true, but then it's hard to sort out the truth in all the jumble. After all, I have been warned about Nora's "uncontrollable fits of violence." Can you imagine Nora trained in the martial arts? Still, I doubt Jeanne would have a problem with Nora taking the classes. Jeanne might be worried about whether or not Nora would sign herself up, manage the payments on the classes, show up for them.

One time, Nora complained that Jeanne wouldn't reschedule an appointment somewhere that Nora had missed. Before the case manager would call for a new appointment, she wanted to talk about why Nora had skipped the old one. Nora didn't want to discuss her reasons, didn't want to be hassled. She believes Jeanne should have just made the new appointment, no questions asked. Nora says she finally told Jeanne to forget about it, she'd make the appointment herself. "Jeanne is manipulative and controlling—just like we are on the street," Nora says.

Another time, Nora complained that Jeanne keeps asking her what she's doing with her money. "I don't ask her what she does with her paycheck, do I?" Nora argues persuasively.

"Maybe Jeanne feels responsible for you. Maybe she's worried you might get hurt, maybe she feels she needs to protect you."

Nora responds, "But I need the trust more."

We arrive at the red brick building that houses a branch of the New York City Department of Health. Nora walks me through, obviously familiar with the place. There are about a dozen people in the waiting area, eyes glued to a video featuring an HIV-infected former addict talking about AIDS prevention. Nora says we need to take a number. Ours is 52. A health worker calls out for patient number 50. I am momentarily encouraged, "Great, our number will be called soon!" Nora laughs at me. First you get a number to wait your turn to sign in, and then you get another number to wait to see the doctor. In the end, we wait about an hour altogether.

An hour is a long time, given that Nora is waiting to hear the results of her HIV test. But it is a short wait, given that we have walked in without an appointment.

Nora is becoming more and more anxious. She says things like, "If I'm positive, I'll probably just want to get high." "If I'm positive, I'll live fifteen years, the most." "If I'm positive, my life is over."

Her nervousness is catching. Before long I find myself expecting the worst. We spend most of the time chitchatting. Nora talks about men with great disdain and hostility. "From now on, I'm going to avoid them altogether and just stick to women," she promises. We talk about the dangers of mixing crack and prescription medications. Nora takes the Thorazine they've given her only occasionally; when she's "drinkin' and druggin'," she forgoes the "meds" altogether.

Nora jumps up to find out when her turn will be and disappears down a hallway. She's next, and they let her into an examining room.

I wait, tap my foot, read pamphlets. The waiting brings back memories: graduate school on Forty-second Street (maybe Nora was across the street in Bryant Park), the big exam, standing in the hallway, staring at some print on the wall, convinced I had failed. I am certain that this time Nora is hearing she's HIV positive. She's been in there five, six, seven, eight, nine, ten minutes and she's still not out.

Finally she's back and sits down, almost casually. "What is it?" I ask. I can't tell from her expression. Nothing yet. They told her to go back out here to wait. They aren't really ready for her. They are busy with somebody else. I feel relieved, but just nod.

Down the hall again. This time, she's gone for only five minutes. She's skipping back with a thumbs-up. I am elated, relieved, so happy. We hug. I'm dying for a bourbon.

4

Sorrow and Melancholia

IN EARLY JANUARY, the Woodhouse library is cluttered with bags filled with donated clothing. There are more goodies at this time of year than at others, a result of the holiday spirit. Most of the time, Dixie is in charge of sorting through and distributing the donations. This season she finds something special for herself—a mink coat, no less. She had always wanted one, and this coat is beautiful and incredibly warm. The fur is tawny and soft and luxurious. The lining is smooth and silky. It doesn't matter that the initials monogrammed on the inside are "ERS."

Dixie's coat is the talk of the house. What a find! She hates to take it off.

On Sunday evening, Dixie and Diane treat themselves to dinner at the Olympic. As it turns out, the coat doesn't even last the weekend.

It starts to shed a little before she leaves the house. A few strands of mink here and there. Still, Dixie is set on wearing her new fur. By the time the two friends arrive at the diner, clumps of mink mark their path through the snow.

Dixie gingerly drapes the coat on the back of her chair in the restaurant. It doesn't matter how careful she is. The coat has fallen apart. Fur covers the floor under her chair. She is disappointed, but it's not that big a deal. She shrugs. "There was nothing to be done about it. I had no choice but to throw it out."

Besides, she tells me, Christmas at Woodhouse was a real treat. Dixie is excited. Usually, the gifts are just awful, but this year, there were presents and presents and presents. Dixie got a new pair of slacks, and they fit just right. There was plenty of other good stuff too, even real perfume.

Dixie and I plan a melt-in-the-mouth stew, perfect for a dreary, ice-cold day like this one in the dead of winter. We get going early to be sure the stew cooks for hours, simmering on a low flame. A collection of cilantro, dill, parsley, and green and yellow vegetables covers the table, and the two of us settle into the task at hand.

"I lived at the Sun Hotel for eight and a half years and loved every minute of it," Dixie begins. "The landlord, an older man, he's dead now. He gave it over to his son. When his son took over, he got into the SRO route and got in with the Olivieri Center and made an SRO hotel. It was bright, sort of rinky, looked like Mother Hubbard's. It was home to me and I liked it there.

"I had a room with a sink, which was marvelous. I was on the third floor. Three bathrooms on each floor, two showers and a tub. I had a room with a sink and that was about it, but I don't know, it was different than here. I used to wash my clothes, hang them on the fire escape to dry, you know, we did all that. All of us, we used to do stuff like that, all of us that lived there.

"And I used to cook, that was my job. Out of forty-two who lived there, I'd make it for fifteen, but you used to pay fifty cents for it though. Supper was at four o'clock in the afternoon, and it was good. There was meat and potatoes and vegetables. I would go shopping every morning to get my food– you know, fresh meat from the butcher, fresh condiments from the store, fresh produce–and make a nice little meal. We'd have our tuna, our canned food also, and stuff the social worker would get from her organization, but in general it was fresh food and people liked it.

"I cooked pork chops and sweet potatoes and apples, baked apples. Spaghetti and meat balls and salad. I would cook a beef stew.

"I learned how to cook when I was young. My mother insisted. I learned all the homemaking things, my mother was very good at it."

Lured by our chatter and the smell of stew, more women begin to gather around the table. "Hi, everybody," Teri announces cheerfully as she enters the library. She is back from Fountain House, a day program she attends for job training and socializing. "You know what I heard today?" Teri asks of nobody in particular. "I heard that Fountain House is building a brand new residence, and it's going to be beautiful. You can have your *own* kitchen."

This last bit of information prompts several women to look up from their thoughts. "Oh yeah?" "Really?" "What'd you hear?" A string of questions comes from the group waiting patiently at the table for their meal.

Teri describes the proposed facility: new and clean with kitchens for all, and the same programs already offered by Fountain House–therapy, independent living, job training.

Dominique's interest is piqued. "Maybe I'll move there," she suggests.

"But you'll have to share a room," Nora points out. Word of the new residence was already old news for Nora.

"I'd like that," Dominique responds. "I *want* to share a

room." Dominique may be thinking about the times she "hears voices" and can't sleep alone. That's when she knocks on her neighbor's door to ask if she can sleep with her.

"Maybe *I'll* move there," says Dixie, as if trying on the idea.

"I'd just as soon stay here," Hattie concludes. These days, Hattie's main concern is "looking to get a job." Her most likely prospect is as a messenger, though this never does pan out. "I'd like to brush up on my secretarial skills," Hattie declares, "and learn how to use a computer." For a dozen years, college-educated Hattie had been a legal secretary, a corporate secretary, and a secretary in a shipping company. That was nearly fifteen years ago, and Hattie knows it's a whole new world today.

Most Woodhouse women with work histories have had service jobs like the ones offered in-house. A couple worked in factories, before these packed up and left town.[1]

Many years ago, for instance, Diane had worked in a couple of factories in the Bushwick section of Brooklyn. One place, Birkencrest, manufactured Halloween costumes and masks. Diane worked there five years before they closed down and she lost her job. As Diane describes it, "the wages weren't high. I earned about seventy dollars a week, but I liked the work. I was a spec on the floor–trimming garments. After they closed up, I went on welfare 'cause I had no job."

Patsy got her first factory job when she was sixteen years old, in Atlanta, Georgia. Her task was to put roach spray in boxes. Patsy didn't last long at this job, the only one she's ever had.

Debra Brown has had several jobs. She's worked "in a supermarket, in a hotel cleaning up, and any kind of job I could get." At one point or another, Sharlea, Lynda, and even Nora have found employment in their local supermarkets. Only Lynda diversified, having worked as a baby-sitter, at

Kentucky Fried Chicken, and for a book company on Water Street, where she did "binding and inserting." In the 1980s, Dresden Comforter held a job for four years as a customer service representative. Susan Jones, who had worked quite some time as a salesgirl for Woolworths, recalls difficulties she has had in finding work over the years.

The problem, according to Susan, is that immigrants are taking jobs away from American workers. "I lost out on a job to this Mexican one time. He laughed at me. He said he got the job and I didn't. It's just like in Germany, the Holocaust. The reason this happened to the Jews was that all the Jews were rich and had taken jobs away from the German people. So the Holocaust happened because people were angry about that."

"I talked to Gary [a case manager] about getting me into some kind of training program too, for typing maybe, or steno," Dixie reports. She sounds weary. "Gary wants me to get a job outside of Woodhouse, but I don't know. He says maybe it's cold feet, but the only thing I could do is clean houses. At this point in my life, I really don't want to dust other people's furniture."

Dominique tells us she expects to get a job in the mail room at Fountain House. "I can keep my SSI as long as I don't make more than two thousand dollars a year," Dominique explains when asked what would happen to her benefits once she starts working. "More than that and they'll take money out of my disability."

"It's sixty-five dollars a month," Nora corrects Dominique. For Nora, "None of that's for me." Instead she's "thinking about getting a permit to sell flowers on the street. I'd be independent, not work for a boss."

Several women are already involved in Woodhouse's work program.[2] Earning one dollar per hour, resident workers have a range of jobs. Diane runs errands for the office.

Many times, she needs to get something to the agency's main office downtown. Diane has been in the work program for five years and averages between fifteen to eighteen hours a week. She describes a typical day. "I work from about six-thirty to eight-thirty in the morning, cleaning, sweeping, mopping. I finish the downstairs around nine o'clock, and then I clean the upstairs floors. Or if the office needs me, I'll deliver messages to the main office. You can make good money here. It's just house pay, but it's hard to find a job that pays minimum wage."

Crystal Howard works the front desk and also performs housework chores in the laundry room and hallways. "Working the front desk" means sitting at the entrance to Woodhouse, buzzing in residents and visitors, and taking and transferring all incoming calls to the house. Several women take turns as receptionists. Others work as house librarians, do kitchen work (clearing trays, washing dishes, cooking and serving food), and housekeeping (cleaning bathrooms, mopping the hallways and kitchen floor, taking out the garbage). Felice Mills is considered the best of all the housekeepers. She always keeps "the bathrooms in spic and span order."

Now, rumor has it, the work program may be eliminated altogether. Nobody knows exactly why. Some say it's because certain women are not doing their job properly. Others say it's about money and budget cuts. Whatever the reason, the general consensus is that eliminating the program would be "terrible," "stupid," "ridiculous."

Crystal was working the front desk the first day I met Patsy's fiance, Joseph. Crystal giggled at the two of us as she rang up for Patsy. Unbeknownst to either of us, Joseph and I are both waiting to see Patsy. "What's so funny?" I ask Crystal. She finally lets on that "Joseph is here to see Patsy too. He's her *boyfriend*."

Joseph shakes my hand eagerly, delighted I will be meeting with his special friend. "Patsy's a wonderful person," he tells me. "I love her." He is here to see Patsy just for a minute, to give her some food—canned goods like ravioli and corn. But I may see her first, he insists, he'll be happy to wait until we are done. "I love Patsy," Joseph tells me again. "When I get situated, you know, financially, I'm gonna marry her."

Crystal cuts in. She has reached Patsy in her room. "Patsy says she can't see you now," Crystal informs Joseph. "She says you can come back later." The model of politeness, Joseph makes a graceful exit: not to worry, come back later, pleased to meet you, good day.

"Joseph is such a gentleman," I tell Patsy as she comes down the stairs to meet with me.

"Yes." Patsy smiles. "We've only been going out for a couple of months but we want to get married."

At thirty-one, Patsy's had a lifetime of trouble with men. This time it's different, because Joseph is respectful and shares with Patsy her "Christian values." If nothing else, Patsy wants me to understand the role she plays at Woodhouse: "I minister the word of God to the ladies here. If you ever need anyone to talk to, I am here. I'd like to help you any way I can. Always, always feel free to knock on my door, and you can talk to me about any problems you may have. *We* don't always have to come to *you* for help, *you* can come to *us* for help too. You know, staff are human too."

In the worst of times, Patsy turned to God to help her through. An orphan, a homeless woman, a mother without her children, Patsy knows about suffering and the healing power of salvation.

Her story begins in Jamaica, Queens, where she was born of a mother institutionalized at Creedmore Psychiatric

Hospital. Patsy was raised by relatives, for whom she cleaned and cooked until she was kicked out of the house for becoming pregnant with her first child.

Patsy details her anguished initiation into motherhood. "I was raped by my first daughter's father. I was fifteen. My daughter's father was thirteen years old when he raped me. I had been dating him, but one day he took me into the basement and he raped me. He hurt me. He put a broom up my vagina. I lost five ounces of blood because of that. His name is Rod Gerson and he got two years in prison for rape and murder. He kills babies."

Patsy says her daughter Sasha Rebecca was conceived in the rape. In all, Patsy has four children, all of them placed in foster care by the Bureau of Child Welfare.

"How old are they now?" I ask.

"I'm not sure," Patsy answers, furrowing her brow as she collects the memories. "Let's see, the youngest must be nine years old by now. Sasha Rebecca was born on July 24, Marisa Pearl was born on July 23, Angel was born on October 24 or 25, and the youngest, Jacob, was born on October 24." Patsy says she had her "tubes tied" after the birth of her fourth child.

And the fathers?

"They were men I went home with, I didn't know them well," answers Patsy, sounding at once distant and wistful. But for a short interval when she lived in Georgia, Patsy spent most of her teenage years and young adulthood in New York, "more or less riding the subways." For a long time, Patsy managed to stay afloat by "being on the trains and where the other homeless people were and following guys home." Patsy frequently sought temporary refuge at city churches, especially the one right by Grand Central Station. It's only been a few short years since Patsy found her way first to a city shelter and now to Woodhouse.

One or two guys Patsy came to know quite well. One was Paco, one of Chris Sliwa's Guardian Angel vigilantes, who protected the subways during the 1980s. Then there was old man, Samuel O'Connell, a "crackhead" who Patsy stayed with for seven years on the street. Patsy herself was never much of a drug user. She'd maybe "smoke a little reefer but that's about it." These days, all that is out of the picture, ever since she's become "a Christian and got close to God."

Overall, Patsy is pretty content at Woodhouse. She knows almost everybody but reserves a special affection for best friend Tanya McNeil and for old acquaintances from their days on the street. For example, Patsy goes way back with Margery and her mother, when the three women frequented the same street corners, subways, and shelters.

Patsy chooses to "keep pretty much to myself." She spends a lot of her time in her room, preferring it to the communal areas such as the cafeteria, dayroom, or library. "Most of the time I watch TV and read the Bible twice a day," Patsy says, "and I make my own meals in my room." Others say Patsy actually "hoards," not "prepares," food in her room, despite having been at Woodhouse for two years. This practice, which staff attribute to Patsy's days of homelessness, causes somewhat of a health hazard at the residence, since Patsy's room is the center of Woodhouse's infestation of roaches and maggots.

Patsy insists her ailments also keep her close to home. Between the high blood pressure, frequent stomach viruses, asthma, and menstrual cramps, Patsy chooses not to venture too far. It wasn't long ago that Patsy recovered from a bout of tuberculosis. "I had TB for a year," Patsy says. "I stayed in the hospital for three months, getting treatment for TB. I coughed a lot and had night sweats."

Nowadays, Patsy is busy planning her upcoming wedding to Joseph. Joseph is a godsend, and Patsy loves their dinner dates at the local pizza parlor or at Kentucky Fried Chicken. She speaks hopefully about her future. "I'm excited about the wedding. It'll be sometime next year, and you're invited. I'll let you know when. I wouldn't want you to miss it for the world. We might be married at Woodhouse, we haven't decided yet. After we get married, we'll try to move to a residence for married people."

For the life of him, though, Joseph is one young man who can't find a job, and it's getting him down. Until he finds work, the couple puts off the wedding. In the meantime, Patsy remains patiently at Woodhouse and Joseph lives with his mother in the Bronx.

Joseph has tried everything, to no avail. In the prime of his life, the thirty-something black man with a "mental disability" has gone by the book, without result. He's gone to all the right "programs," but still no job. He's followed the advice of counselors, therapists, and case managers, but still no job. It is no wonder Joseph is in despair. As he shares with me his struggle to just get by, Joseph can't help letting the anger show.

He tells me that the programs are ultimately "demeaning." If they can't help you get a job, what's the use? Joseph says he gets nothing but "the runaround." His counselors insist he continue in their "programs." Joseph just wants to get a job.

"I'm not a child, I'm a man," he says simply. All he wants is to marry Patsy, provide for her, and move out of his mother's house. Joseph hopes to set up housekeeping with his beloved. "I love her, and she's a grown woman too," he maintains, as if he's been told otherwise.

Even his relationship with Patsy "worries" his counselor, according to Joseph, "They don't respect me." Again Joseph insists, "I'm an adult."

They keep telling him to continue with school, get more

training. "That's demeaning to me too 'cause I've been in
school long enough," Joseph repeats. "I'll tell you this," he
says, "I don't want a janitor job. I want an office job. I can
do it. I can answer phones. I can file things. I can talk to
people."

It's been almost a year now since Patsy and Joseph told me
of their plans. The couple is as tight as ever. Joseph is still
looking for work. One evening I see them stroll into Woodhouse arm in arm. Joseph is holding their new "baby," a doll
named Lulubug.

"How's it going with the job search?" I ask Joseph.

"So-so," he answers solemnly. "I might have a job behind
the counter at Burger King."

At least he got an interview, but he hasn't heard yet
whether he's landed the position. Joseph goes on, "I hope
I got the job 'cause I want to marry Patsy and I worry about
supporting her. And we're looking for housing before the
wedding."

Joseph and Patsy remind me of a story Tanya once wrote:

This is a Story about Middle and Poor Class People

There once was a woman named Sandy who married
Andy. After a while, Sandy got pregnant with her first
child. While she was still pregnant, she got a job to try
to make ends meet. After a while had passed, she was
thinking what things would be like if she hit the lotto.

While she was thinking about lotto, she thought about
getting a better place to live, but it just wouldn't happen.
So Andy told Sandy how can you think about having kids
and we have no where to go?

Then one day, Sandy had a dream and it suddenly
came true. She played lotto and she won. So Sandy told
Andy that some day your dreams will come true too. So
they bought a house after she hit the lotto for
$10,000,000,000 a good amount of money. They all lived

happily ever after, even though they totally forgot what happend.

Patsy comes to stand by her fiancé. She slips her arm around his. "He's had a lot of disappoints," she explains sympathetically. "He has to trust Jesus and be patient. All the things he wants will happen in time—an apartment, get married, have a baby."

"Bless you," Patsy wishes me good-bye as she and Joseph head upstairs to her room.

5

Abuses of the Spirit

D<small>ENISE</small> S<small>COTT</small> is working the reception desk. It's
a surprise to see her sitting still; most often she is on the
go. Denise greets me with a gummy smile, her teeth lost to
the streets. Today, her naturally coiled hair is unnaturally
slicked down with pomade. Leaning over the counter, I
catch a whiff of whiskey and ask about her daughter.

Denise places her hand on her own slim belly, pushing it
out. Renee is pregnant.

Denise describes her only child as "an active crack
abuser." Renee already has three children and now she's
pregnant again. Denise hoped it wouldn't be so. She wishes
her daughter would have an abortion, but Renee reminds
her mother that abortion is against their religion. "We're
Catholic," Denise explains as she raises an eyebrow, perhaps thinking about her daughter's religious convictions.

"My daughter wants to go into recovery," Denise explains,
"but she doesn't know how to get started. Who's going to
take care of the kids? She's abused them in the past. She's
worried about losing them. Now she's getting high every
day."

Two of Renee's three children were born crack-addicted,
according to Denise.

Denise is a longtime resident of Woodhouse, but her drinking problems may end her streak of decent housing luck. Three years ago, Denise had the chance to move to Georgia with her longstanding boyfriend Alfred. She didn't go, she says, because she knows Renee needs her to be nearby, as does her aged mother. The old lady is confined to her one-room apartment some blocks north in Harlem. Denise visits often and brings her little things she needs. Most often, Renee comes by Woodhouse on Saturdays and brings the kids to visit with their grandma Denise. In the meantime, Alfred remains patient, calling Denise every few months to see if she has changed her mind. She hasn't.

DEBRA BROWN doesn't seem worried about wearing out her welcome at Woodhouse. She insists she doesn't have a drug problem. Maybe she's one of the women Victoria describes as "in complete denial," at least when it comes to drugs.

"Crack's a nice little high," is Debra's position. "I've been a crack and reefer user for about five years now." Debra, with her velvety, chocolate-colored skin and model-like cheekbones, is one of the few women at Woodhouse who has a youthful appearance. Without the bandanna she wears over cropped hair and minus the back-and-forth rocking movements inspired, most probably, by Prolixin, you might consider Debra elegant.

Debra tells me that "the people at Woodhouse" don't want her to do crack anymore, but she thinks it's okay. "It doesn't seem like it harms you, and it's a nice little high," Debra says in almost a whisper.

"They don't let you smoke crack in here," she informs me.

"Why?" I ask.

"'Cause they put you out."

Debra is matter-of-fact about any and all details of her life. She had her first taste of alcohol and cigarettes when she was fourteen years old. Her mother died of cancer when she was eleven, but it didn't matter much because Debra had been living in foster care anyway since she was seven. For some of the time, she had lived with one aunt in Brooklyn and another in Ohio. Debra's father died when she was seven years old, and her older brother Trevor died "of alcohol" too. She has another brother someplace. His name is James.

Debra moved to Ohio just before she was to enter high school. Her aunt Mary invited her to come because she had only sons and had always wanted a daughter. Debra didn't mind. In Ohio, she went to school up to the tenth grade.

When she was fourteen, Debra had a baby boy. His name is Martin, and he's now twenty-two years old. The only other time Debra became pregnant was when she was about eighteen, but she had an abortion. After that, she took birth control pills for about three years and never became pregnant again. She believes the birth control pills "just stuck to me, stuck to my ribs," from the time she started taking them until now.

One time, Debra was hospitalized for "mental illness," but she doesn't know "what kind" of mental illness. She remembers walking into the emergency room of a hospital. She says she just stayed there and wouldn't leave, so they "committed me."

The nurse at Woodhouse gives Colgentin and Prolixin to Debra every day. Debra says the only bad side effect of these pills is "they make me fat."

When some guy told her that her "pussy stinks," Debra started to use Massengill douche. She went over to the Ryan Center for a checkup. They told her she had syphilis and treated her with penicillin.

They also told her she was HIV positive. Debra says she

felt "okay" when they gave her this news. "I'll be dying soon," she says quietly. "I'm not afraid because I have nothing to be afraid of."[1]

Unlike Debra, Dixie can't understand crack's appeal. "High for fifteen minutes, then have to come back and get another high for fifteen minutes, and another high for fifteen minutes—forget about it. I think it's a cheap thrill, and I don't go for it. High for ten minutes, what kind of crap is that? Maybe I shouldn't talk about cheap thrills, but to me, I got high and not for fifteen minutes." Years ago, Dixie had a morphine habit.

"I was living in Louisiana. My parents had died when I was eleven. Both of them had heart attacks. I was living with one of my aunts in Louisiana.

"When I started using drugs, I was about sixteen. I got a hold of morphine at the docks. I was by myself and I was on the docks and I was out for the weekend and I just started taking drugs. Injecting. It was morphine, not heroin.

"I did this on the weekends, and during the week I went to school. It took six months to catch a good habit. And then I was addicted. And then I ran out of money so I had to un-addict myself because I couldn't afford it. I was eighteen.

"It was rough. Cold, nose running all the time, it still does. Stomach cramps. I was about twenty-three before I was finished. I never went back to it. I never wanted any other kind of high. I couldn't afford the morphine, and I wasn't gonna get into any other kind of high.

"The morphine took away all the pain, of losing my parents, that also. It just made me feel good, the pain in my heart."

Over the years, Dixie also developed a taste for alcohol. She says, "I form habits easily, very easily." For Dixie, "It started out I was going with someone who drank, and then it became a daily thing." It has been very difficult to give it up. "The stopping process is horrible. Worse than drugs, if you ask me." Dixie sees it this way: "It's so accessible, and you always have the money for it. It's right there in the grocery store. You pass it every day. You see it every day. You gotta be involved with this somehow every day, for one reason or another.

"Whenever I'm bored, I want a beer. I've got nothing to do.

"To get yourself a wine cooler, all you have to do is go around the corner to the grocery store. Who is going to stop you? You have to stop yourself."

SUSAN SMITH has one eye on the bottle and the other on making "a move higher for myself." As we head upstairs to her room, Susan, better known around here as "Smithy," tells me she's set to move out of Woodhouse for another residence in the Bronx, the borough where she was born.

The climb is up four flights of stairs, no easy task for Smithy, whose short, delicate frame can't readily maneuver the dozens of extra pounds it carries. To catch her breath, the forty-year-old white woman lingers on the landing between each floor. After each flight, she has a new pretext for stopping. One time, Smithy adjusts the lavender pant legs pulled tight around her thighs. On the next landing, she takes a small comb to pull back wisps of graying hair from her small face. At the top, she searches for her key inside the pocketbook she carries properly on her forearm.

Smithy's room is in the central corridor of the building. The dusty room has little fresh air and no natural light. Smithy tries to keep it bright with her Barbie doll castle, several plastic Santas, and puppy dog stickers that cover each dresser drawer and closet door. She fills the room with country music, her favorite kind, and proudly displays her new radio.

Smithy is so nervous about her upcoming interview at the new place, she can barely concentrate on our conversation. She fondly remembers a similar meeting at Woodhouse: "When I came here for my interview, I came through Victoria, and I had my interview. As I was leaving that same day, Victoria asked me, 'What color do you want your room?' She asked me what color do I want for my room.

"I said pink."

Smithy grew up being called "retarded," a label she rejects because "a retarded person can't do the things I do, like quilting afghans, or being on your own since you're seventeen years old."

Like Dixie, Smithy moved to Coney Island when she found herself on her own. A teenager at the time, Smithy chose that famous Brooklyn spot "because of the rides."

"At the beginning, people used to throw pennies out, when they used to see me. And I used to pick them up. All their pennies. But then I met some people, out working down there. I was out working on the games and all. I worked with the games, like Bust the Balloon—you know, putting the balloons up, every time when they was broken.

"For a while I was on the street. And then I found a hotel, seeing that I was getting paid. I met a lot of people and they used to watch out for me.

"I was eighteen when I started drinking."

THESE DAYS, she tries to drink coffee instead of J&B and Coke. This explains why Smithy is always off to the deli with her best buddy, Susan Jones. The two have been fast friends since meeting at 350 Lafayette. Smithy's move will be hard on them, but it's what she needs to do for herself.

Susan Jones slowly strokes the cover of a magazine while she speaks fondly of her father, who is deceased. The family had its share of hardships, especially since money was tight and Susan's mother suffered from schizophrenia. As she talks about the family, her puffy hands move sometimes rapidly, sometimes slowly, over the slick paper, depending on who she is talking about. If about her father, Susan's gestures and voice soften. If about her mother, Susan bristles and her hands wave around furiously. Of her parents, Susan says bitterly, "My father worked very hard. My mother was a good person, but unfortunately, her illness sometimes made her do cruel things." Most of the cruelty was directed at the husband, who, Susan explains, "believed the old fashioned thing, be the provider for the wife." It saddens Susan to think of her mother's cruelty. To her saga of sin and redemption, Susan offers this ending: "My mother, when she was dying, she straightened her mind out for a few minutes, and she said to me, 'Your father was good to me and I hurt him.'"

As Susan chronicles the family history, sometimes the story jumps centuries, sometimes decades: "My makeup is English and French, German and Irish.[2] My father's family was French and English. Come from upstate, family been in this country generations. Had relatives in the Civil War. My mother's people were in America during the time of the Revolution. My mother was German and Irish. She was in the hospital, in and out a lot of times. All different hospitals in Manhattan and Queens. She's made the grand tour. And then I came to Woodhouse."

In between were years of labor and sickness. Most of the time, the setting was Manhattan's West Village. During those years, Susan's father worked for Henry Hardy's Candy Company, which manufactured jelly beans and chocolates sold under names like Barricini and Whitman's.

Susan's father was the "floor man" at the factory, so he got to bring home boxes of candy. "They made really good chocolates," Susan remembers, "and marshmallow. Ruined my baby teeth."

The sequence of events is unclear. Susan remembers that the factory closed down and moved to New Jersey. At one point, her father worked as a doorman for a fancy Manhattan apartment building. At another point, the family was evicted from their Greenwich Village home. Susan doesn't know why. She remembers the four of them–father, mother, daughter, and son–sitting on a bench with Charlie, the family dog, in Sheridan Square. Susan was eight years old and it was wintertime, February. A kindly police officer approached the family. The officer sent them to a hotel and gave them ten dollars for food.

The first hotel wouldn't take them in. "You're a family, only riff-raff are here," Susan recalls the manager saying. He sent them to a better place, with a better class of clientele. The family stayed for five months before finding their own apartment in Brooklyn. Susan says, "My father was earning fifty dollars a week and the hotel cost fifty dollars a week, so a priest gave us money for food."

Susan's mother never got off her husband's back. She constantly berated him, this hardworking family man who would come home from a long day's work to shop and prepare the evening meal. She called him names like "stupid" and accused him of having affairs. She taunted him, telling him she was having an affair. She showed him costume jewelry she claimed her lover had given her. "It was a lie," Susan says. "She'd go out and buy the jewelry herself."

"My father had a very sad life," Susan continues. "He used to take the stress from the bosses in work and then he would come to stress with my mother. He'd have to come home and wash the diapers, do the dishes, take care of us kids. He used to sweep and mop the floors on weekends. He never had time to really rest. He'd come home from work, watch his cowboys, and then go to sleep. The next day, he'd be up, six o'clock in the morning, get ready for work. And all my mother would do all day is sit around the house and tell him what a no-good he was and how she had to push him to work or he wouldn't support us. She hurt him all the time.

"She and pretty much every body else drove him into an early grave. He was only sixty-one when he died. He had cancer and his heart condition was very bad.

"My mother was a good woman, but she had an illness. And the illness made a lot of anger and hurt in the family. I told my father that there was no need to be living with this all the time. Put her in the hospital so they can make her at least well enough to function. My father wouldn't listen to me. And then when he was dying, he said, 'You know, you were right.'

"My father died worrying about my mother. My mother used to do things to him that were very spiteful. When he was in the hospital, he wanted her to come and see him, and she wouldn't go near him.

"It was her illness. She'd be nice and kind and sweet and loving and then all of a sudden she'd get mad and start yelling and finding fault with everything. The only one stuck with Momma at the end, when she was sick, was me. She died in 1989. Of cancer. She had cancer all through her body. Even though we had our fights and disagreements, I still stuck with her. My brother walked out and wouldn't even come back to bury her. He wouldn't even come back to help me get money to bury her. I had to go to my friend, who made arrangements with the Presbyterian Church to bury my mother."

It's been more than a year since Crystal's father died, but she still finds it hard to believe he's really gone. She needs to talk about it often. Talking helps to get it out of her system. All the while, Crystal fiddles with the heavy metallic charms hanging from her earlobes and around her neck. Her father was good to her and she misses him. She tells the story over and over again of when, how, where she received the news of his passing.

"I took my father's death very hard. At first I thought it was a joke, I thought they was joking with me. I was here, and Jeanne and Victoria, they took my fiance, Raymond, to the office. All I could remember was that they were holding him there and I couldn't understand why they was holding him there. It was because they had bad news to tell me. My father died. Raymond kept saying, 'Come on, I'm going to take you to your mother's house.' I've repeated this story thousands of times. He kept saying, 'Crystal, I'm gonna take you to your mother's house because you know we have something to tell you.' By the time we got to my mother's house, I saw all the people writing an obituary."

Crystal proudly shows off her father's obituary and a leaflet given out at the funeral service. The leaflet describes Crystal's father as a good husband, father, and member of the Bronx community where he lived and worked. Crystal says her father was sick with "everything–asthma, bronchitis, trouble breathing," but it was "stress" he succumbed to. At least that's Crystal's opinion. According to his daughter, the fifty-six-year-old man "was a lawyer and an accountant and an insurance broker. He had a lot of positions."

DRESDEN WALKS into the library to put some groceries away in the kitchen area. She has special kitchen privileges and is one of a handful of residents who know the combination for the lock on the refrigerator. Dresden is keenly psychological and political. Her moods run hot and cold, but she is always quick to invent creative solutions when residents arrive at a standstill over one issue or another. In fact, it was Dresden's idea to start the community meeting, a once-a-month session at which residents try to resolve among themselves problems otherwise handled by the administration.

Dresden looks fabulous today. A vegetarian, she also keeps in shape by exercising at the local Jack Lalanne spa. This black woman in her late fifties looks years younger, and today wears a white seashell in her dreadlocks. She's an actress, with a recent off-Broadway production under her belt. Explaining her youthful appearance, Dresden says, "It's because I am true to myself in the way I live my life."

Dresden knows there will be more and more work for her in the near future. She has an agent now and is getting called for auditions. Just a few days ago, she auditioned for a television commercial. Dresden is certain she didn't land that job, because it is past the twenty-four-hour callback that is usual for these things. In the past, this sort of rejection would throw Dresden into a depression. Rejection would be followed by days of beating herself up about it and feeling terrible. This time is different. This time, Dresden isn't torturing herself, isn't questioning everything about her *self.*

Dresden describes a recent visit with her eighty-something-year-old father. She amazed herself at how well she was able to keep him at arm's length. "My father is extremely controlling," Dresden says, "and he believes that when people come to see him, it's only because they want something from him, like money." On this visit, Dresden tried sharing with him her hopes and dreams, but she doubts he heard any of it. Referring to his controlling modus operandi, she says, "Not surprising, my father was a community leader in Brooklyn."

Her father has a live-in companion who stays with him despite his dictatorial ways. Dresden "appreciates" Bess for "staying with him," although the old man shows her no respect or kindness. Dresden offers some examples from this last visit. Coming in from the outside, Bess was having trouble with her key at the door. Dresden and her father were inside the house. It was only a matter of minutes, maybe seconds. By the time Bess worked it out and got herself in, she was cowering in fear as if expecting a reprimand or worse from the old man. Later, when Bess called him to dinner, the man of the house took his time coming to the table. As Dresden tells it, he just waited upstairs, knowing that the meal was served and getting cold on the table. He came down when "he felt like it." Silently, Bess reheated the meal and served it once again. By then, Dresden had already finished eating. She made a point of enjoying the dinner the first time Bess announced it was served.

"It's unfair to the human spirit," Dresden says of these patriarchal abuses.

Nora says she wants to begin her story, "'Life with Father,' from the very beginning when I was a little tiny tot, when I remember my first Christmas.

"I was born in October, which means I'm a devastatin' Scorpio. We're the most sexy sign of the Zodiac. I'm very proud of that, though I don't look at myself as being sexy, other people do. We're also extremely determined and have a lot of strong character traits. My weaknesses are that I can be an extremist in a lot of various ways.

"When I was little I remember the Christmas I had with my family that was made up of my father, my mother, my brothers, and my sisters. We were all there, this Christmas. We lived in the Bronx, in the projects, on the eleventh floor.

"My father was working in a hospital as a janitor, which he hated. He was not very proud of that. He was a very an-

gry man. When he used to come home from work, he was
extremely angry and enraged. He used to tell about how
people treated him on the job.

"My father was very, very fair skinned, coal-black straight
hair and a very handsome guy. One day I asked my mother
why did she marry him, because he seemed so mean. And
she said, 'Because I thought your father reminded me of
Clark Gable.' And she said, 'What a mistake I made,' because he turned out to be a tyrant. He ended up being extremely hostile and abusive. Towards the end of my story,
you'll find out.

"My mother was a registered nurse. She did her nursing
at Mt. Sinai Hospital on Fifth Avenue. She would come home
and she was tired from sixteen hours on the job. I felt a lot
of compassion for my mother because she worked very
hard. My father was having a lot of trouble because he got
out of school in the fifth grade, so he was having a lot of
trouble with himself and with the world.

"That was the last Christmas I ever seen in my household. After that it seemed my whole family, my family life,
fell apart. After that, all hell broke loose.

"My mother was sitting on the couch one day, and my father was wrestling with her. I heard my mother say, 'Please,
stop, stop it.' From that little picture, I noticed that my father
was moving to get physical with my mother.

"I have to say this also. I thought my mother had long
hair, but she did not. She had her hair braided up under a
wig, a red, long wig. She wore this long, straight, reddish-
brown hair at the time. My father had told me, 'The reason
why I married your mother is because when I first met her,
I seen her and she looked like an orange something.' Her
skin was orange and her hair was red, so he right away drew
to this woman. My father was very fair skinned. He didn't
want his kids to be dark. One of my brothers is dark, and my

father would always be on him about that. You know, you
take all these little things, these details into consideration. My
father also goes to the Indians. That's why my mother and my
father named my baby sister Cree. He's from the North and
she's from the South.

"All hell broke loose because my father started drinking,
because of his job. He hated his job. He hated people on it.
He was not very proud of working as a janitor. He just hated
it. He hated it because my mother was a nurse and he was a
janitor. It was demeaning to him because he was a man. It
made him feel bad. It didn't make him feel he was the man
of the house.

"My mother, on the other hand, was from a middle-class,
upper-class family. I guess he felt that she was the stronger
one. So he started drinking and he started becoming very
mean, very abusive. He would use bad language. He would
call my mother names when she would come home from
work, say that she was with somebody when she wasn't. She
had a very bad experience from him.

"One time I witnessed that he picked up a chair, threw
some canned food at her, picked up a chair, and hit her over
the head with a chair. That's when I was about seven or
eight. A couple of times I watched him beat her, punch her.
She would come home from work and he would wrestle
with her. It got so bad, her wig would come off her head.

"I felt terribly bad and I didn't know what to do. I was
afraid of my father by then. I was just afraid, so I started
writing. I couldn't talk to my father or my mother about
what was going on, so I would go in my room, close the
door, and cry when they were fighting. I had these locked
diaries, and I locked 'em and I'd write in them and I'd cry.

"My father didn't take to me well, and I didn't take to
him either. He hurt all of us. His drinking escalated, and
he became more abusive. Okay, now my mother was very,

very frightened of him. She would stay at the hospital so she could get some sleep and she wouldn't come home. So then we were left with him in the house by ourselves.

"One day I was alone in the house by myself and I was afraid. I did something wrong, so he said. He called me in the living room and he took off his big, thick garrison belt he wore. He took the belt off and he whipped me, whipped me, whipped me, and I thought I would die. When my father whipped, he's out of control. He doesn't know when to stop. I thought I was going to die in the midst of this. The buckle had hit me in the eye so I wound up with a black eye.

"When he was finished with me, I went in my room and I lied down in the bed and I cried. When my mother finally came home that evening, I was still in the bed crying. I fell asleep. I was still whimpering in my sleep.

"My mother came in the room. She didn't wake me up. She put the covers over me. I really wanted my mother to pick me up and hold me and call the cops on this man and tell them that he nearly killed me. My father could have killed me. She didn't. I know my mother was extremely afraid of my father, even to the point of her children. That disturbed me a lot. It hurt me a lot. I grew angry at my mother. She didn't talk to me about it, not to this day.

"I became very withdrawn. I wouldn't talk a lot, and I kept to myself. I didn't like going home from school. Who the hell wants to go home to that?

"One of the cruel things that my father did is that once we brought a fruit basket home–big, giant fruit basket with the colored cellophane and ribbons. Well, my brother and I went in it and took the fruits out and ate it. Well, he woke up and he went into a tantrum. Instead of whipping us, he made us eat all the fruit in the basket, or he tried to. By the time we were trying to finish it, he decided to go out. He was getting dressed. We were lucky that he was going out. He told us we didn't have to eat no more. But by the time we got that, we were very, very sick. We lived on the eleventh floor, so we opened the window and spit the food out, vomited the food out, threw it out the window, the fruit. I still sometimes have the pain in my stomach.

"My mother starts bouncing from place to place to place to escape my father, dragging us all along. We're moving from place to place to place, and we finally got a place on Myrtle Avenue in Brooklyn. She's supporting everybody. She's growing meaner and bitter for the kids, for having all these kids, and for having to be put through all this. She's moving, trying to get away from him. He follows her down the line. The abuse is still to continue.

"He's following her and still coming into the picture. She allowed him back in. My father goes out one night, and early one rainy morning the bell rings downstairs. I goes downstairs to open the door. When I open the door, his whole face is full of blood and it scared the living shit out of me. I ran upstairs to my mother. 'Mommy, dad is hurt–his face is full of blood.' He was drinking. He comes upstairs and my mother gets him and sits him down and gets him cleaned up and tells him again about his drinking and tries to talk to him again.

"He still doesn't listen. A couple of weeks later, I woke up one day, came out of my room, and I heard this choking sound, someone choking. I go into the kitchen. I opened the door slowly. My father had my mother against the wall, off the ground, choking her real hard, I mean he was into it real deep. She was really choked. She was actually up off the ground. I jumped on his back and I was pulling him. I jumped all over his back, and I'm pulling. Finally she helps me and she yanks his hand away from her, and she runs out the door. She runs out the door. He knocks me down and goes somewhere in the back.

"All I could do was sit there, and all I could do is cry.

"After that, I grew very extremely sad. I hated people. I didn't know what to think of my family. I didn't know what to think of men. I started to have men issues. I was striking out at boys. I wanted to kill them. I had feelings of just total, total hatred for guys. And meanness. I just wanted to lash out at somebody. I really wanted to lash out at my father. I wanted to kill him. It's a miracle that I did not hurt anyone. I did get into fights with guys, 'cause I wanted to kill them. If they said anything to me the wrong way, if they hit me, I was off. And guys thought I was a crazy, crazy woman.

"I was fifteen, sixteen years old. I was still in school. But I was still a loner, antisocial, which only made my feelings even worse. I felt alienated, I felt isolated. I was in bad shape mentally. I knew it, and I was even scared of my own self. By now I'm having feelings of rage and I didn't know what to do with it. That's when I turned to drinkin' and druggin'."

IT SEEMS NORA has no sense of belonging to anything larger than her dysfunctional family of origin, yet she has managed to survive a lifetime of physical and verbal abuse as well as a series of "personal failures." Having spent the past half decade in the housing system for the mentally ill, as well as in various substance abuse programs, Nora has also had considerable exposure to the common psychological practices of the day. The emphasis on family systems institutionalized in these practices has brought Nora a few steps outside her self; not surprisingly, in those settings, the connection between Nora's "low self-esteem" and the gendered, racialized, and class nature of her experience has never been drawn, though she hints at it.

The way I see it, Nora embodies race, gender, and class in

the United States. A poor black woman, she was not simply raised in a dysfunctional family but is a child of America, where men are shamed if they are less educated than their wives, or if they work at the lowest rung of the social ladder. Years ago, Richard Sennett and Jonathan Cobb described men like Mr. Gaines who have "the feeling of not getting anywhere despite one's efforts, the feeling of vulnerability in contrasting oneself to others at a higher social level, the buried sense of inadequacy that one resents oneself for feeling." These feelings the authors describe as "the burden of class in society" (1972:58). In the following passage, Sennett and Cobb portray one subject in their study of the working class. Ricca, like Nora's father, was a janitor and overwhelmed by a sense of inadequacy.

> It is difficult for Ricca, even as he creates some measure of material security in his life, to feel that his quantitative gains translate into the emotional sense of independence and assuredness he wants from these material improvements. He sees himself as receiving the ultimate form of contempt from those who stand above him in society: he is a function, "Ricca the janitor," he is part of the woodwork. He feels vulnerable and inadequately armed, but what has he done wrong? (1972:50)

Nora's father could not escape these feelings, not even in his own home, where his wife served as a constant reminder of his inferiority because of her family background and her profession. His rage was only partially internalized; most of it was directed at his wife or the children. The rest he swallowed with shots of whiskey.

Of course, being a black man in a white world made matters worse, even if he was "very fair skinned, with straight black hair." Mr. Gaines was "drawn" to his wife-to-be by her "orange skin and red hair," which turned out to be false. Proud of his "Indian" heritage, he named a daughter "Cree" but "got on" a son for being "dark." Mr. Gaines did not create society's divisions; he learned them well, and they *became* him.

As Nora advises, "take all these little things, these details into consideration," and we can begin to understand her rage. Again, Audre Lorde captures it well: "Women of Color in america have grown up within a symphony of anger, at being silenced, at being unchosen [sic], at knowing that when we survive, it is in spite of a world that takes for granted our lack of humanness, and which hates our very existence outside of its service" (1984:129).

No wonder drugs and alcohol play a part in these worlds of suffering. While our media and most "scientific" reports focus on the latest drug of choice (from alcohol to heroin to cocaine to crack to heroin to coke to alcohol), we are fed enormous doses of trivia, and human suffering still goes unnoticed. They teach us all about "those" people behaving badly and irresponsibly and ignore the international political economy of illegal drugs and its role in our city's economy, not to mention the alcohol industry and target marketing (Waterston 1993; Maynard 1995). Poor people's encounters with the criminal justice system also render their substance abuse more visible than that of the privileged, who may mask it behind Betty Ford clinics and the like.

That substance abuse is prevalent in our society is not surprising–only that it is not more prevalent. As I hear the words of those at Woodhouse who are or have been alcohol and street-drug abusers, pain and its counterpoison come together. Dixie says, "The morphine took away all the pain of losing my parents . . . the pain in my heart." Of crack, Nora says, "It's pure pleasure, peace, contentment." She seeks this antidote (pleasure, peace, contentment) only after her pain has become unbearable.

"Fragmentation and divisions of the self," Sennett and Cobb observe, "are the arrangements consciousness makes in response to an environment where respect is not forth-coming as a matter of course" (1972: 214).

6

Love and Other Intimacies

THIS IS THE day I have a date with Sonia Morales, who well fits the description of a woman "at high risk" for HIV infection, if she isn't already infected.[1] Most of the time, Sonia walks around in a stoned haze, probably from the street drug she regularly inhales. I can't find the small, frail woman anywhere around the house, and nobody has seen her since the morning.

Nora hasn't seen her either. "It's hard to catch someone who's running," Nora explains, and I realize it's time to give up the search for Sonia. "If I was running in the street, you wouldn't be able to catch me either," Nora warns.

This day, Nora feels great. She attended the Gay March held in Central Park this weekend. "Everybody was serene– even the cops," Nora reports, "It reminds me of the old pictures of the civil rights movement, but without the cops spraying water on everybody. There was an amazing amount of people and everybody kept peaceful."

Around Woodhouse, though, the talk has mostly been about O. J. Simpson and murder. "Why do so many men do that?" Nora wants to know. Finding many parallels to her own life, Nora finds the whole thing too upsetting to discuss. "I know he killed his wife," she concludes.

Nora and I organize the cooking group for the day. We plan to boil up some pasta and make a salad. Together we go marketing on Broadway. Nora is in the mood for a lobster sauce, but we can't find any in Key Foods. She settles for clams, and we decide the menu will be spaghetti with clam sauce, garlic bread, sliced tomatoes, onion and avocado, and watermelon for dessert. I've got my eye on a couple of special spots on Broadway where Sonia is known to panhandle—Kentucky Fried Chicken, Academy Florist, Chemical Bank. Nora brings up a new subject.

"You know, I think sometimes society has gotten us in a lot of trouble with labels, that's how I feel. They'da screwed us up," she laughs.

Nora finds blind acceptance of social norms difficult. In words and deed, and in how she tells her own story, Nora is always questioning. In her searches for identity, I recall how Nora tries on an array of gender styles: "All the women who go with big-shot guys were dressing in heels, talk smart, outside her lip . . . [at] that time my hair was longer, and I wore lipstick, makeup and heels and dresses and pant suits and my minks and my rings . . . . I was [Charlie's] woman, so I was always by his side." Shortly after she fit that description, Nora changed gears and enlisted in the armed forces.

Today she's talking about race.

"They label us black, but I don't call myself black. I call myself mixed, you know?" Nora takes up the challenge to surrender those "artificial boundaries that divide an unruly world into tidy analytic chambers" (Kleinman, Das, and Lock 1996: xiii). She *is* the "crack between our categories."

Nora goes on. "And they label people 'white,' and I don't know where they got that from. I think they just botched us up. I think society has botched us up with all this stuff. It's caused people a lot of problems with each other." But without "race," how would we know who to exclude and marginalize? "The fatal coupling of difference and power" is Stuart Hall's description of the core of racism and the work it does in welcoming some while relegating others to the dustbin. Perhaps the ultimate image of the racialized other, blacks in the United States represent that which is to be most feared. Once again, fear is projected onto an-other, arrived there by "all that symbolic and narrative energy and work [that] secures us 'over here' and them 'over there,' fixes each in its appointed species place" (1992:15–16). To help suppress and control that which is different is good reason to keep the labels; danger must be contained.

Nora rejects the label "black" though she embodies it too. "I call myself mixed. I am mixed. My mix is this. My father's great-grandfather was white. Now my father was very fair skinned, very fair skinned, straight black hair. My father also goes to the Indians, down the line. My mother, on the other hand, she doesn't talk about her ancestors too much. My father did. All I know about my mother's side is that they were 'masons,' whatever the hell that is. I don't know what no 'mason' is."

I offer a suggestion, "People who work in cement, building, concrete?"

"No," Nora sees I am way off track. "When I was a little girl, I saw this big guy with all these medals on. He wore this uniform. I asked my mother, 'What, what is granddaddy?'" And my mother would turn to me and say, 'Your grandfather is a high-ranking mason.' So I wondered, what is a mason? And to this day I don't know. I do not know. Maybe I'll go to the library and find out 'What is a mason?'" This turn in the conversation has us both laughing. There is pleasure in the absurdity and neither of us wants it to stop.

"Oh," I laugh, "I thought you meant works in cement, you know, a mason, does masonry–but I don't think he would need a uniform! So it's an organization–the Masons and the Elks."

"Yeah, yeah. He must have been high top because he had all these medals all over, all over his hat, all over his chest. Yeah, I heard the Elk word, and so my grandfather was one of them."

Nora's critique of social labels applies to her notion of sexuality as well as race. For herself, Nora is refreshingly straightforward: "I just feel that my sexuality, sometimes I like women, to be around women, and be intimate with women, sometimes. Sometimes I like it with men too. So I guess in this world, they would call me bisexual. I'm not serious with that. If I like somebody, I love somebody, that's it."

If it were only that simple. At times, Nora is little concerned about what to call herself. For her, the deeper struggle is in the relationship, something she feels still eludes her. Other times, Nora seems to feel utterly alone with her thoughts. Overwhelmed by exclusion, she begins to wonder what is wrong with her self. At these times, Nora comes to believe she is "queer," a "freak," just as the world says. The damage done, Nora becomes open to abuse by others and herself.

Nora taps on the table as she talks about it.

"To this day I have problems with sex and stuff like that, you know. It's hard for me to be intimate. It's hard to be serious about it. I'm still not mature a little bit. Sometimes I guess you have fun with sex. I guess I still know there's a serious part to it, an intimate part of it which I'm not in tune with. Hopefully down the line, in the years to come down the line, maybe I can run into someone I can truly trust and who can trust me and we would have a *re-la-tion-ship,* not because of sex, but a relationship unto each other. You know, sex would be involved, but it won't be the top priority. That's what I want, that's what I'm looking for."

Nora describes two great loves in her life. One was Tommy, one Mabel.

"I had fallen in love first when I had gotten pregnant by Tommy. I was probably about fifteen, fourteen, thirteen, fourteen, fifteen years old, still living with my mother. I was shy, and I loved this guy because he was so handsome. I always wondered, why did this guy, why does this young boy, why does he want somebody like me, 'cause I was shy and plain Jane. I had no idea why he would like a person like me. My mother never gave me any reason to like myself, so I didn't know.

"I adored this guy. He had wavy, sandy hair. Still to this day, I attract handsome little guys. This guy had wavy hair. He had hazel brown eyes and fair skin. I said, 'Man, what a dream boat,' and I go extreme about this guy. But I was so insecure and so shy, he always said to me, 'Why you never talk?'

"One day we were in a park somewhere. I forgot where we had sex, but we had it. I got very terrified, so I got up some money and went and had an abortion somewhere on the East Side. I got rid of the child and that was the end. There was no more Tommy because, by our moving around so much, I've lost him. So my heart broke again, so it made me sad again.

"I tended to get men that were abusive, men I didn't like. I was extremely afraid, and I was afraid to tell them, 'I don't like you,' and I was afraid to get away from them. I allowed them to have over me and stuff like that at times.

"Then I ran into Marcus. Marcus was a banker, he did numbers in the street, and he had plenty of money and cars and he liked me. One day I decided to go on my own–that's when the independence started to come out of me. Then one day I decided to be a little bit independent, work for a lady baby-sitting. 'Why did I do that for?' he called me down-stairs. Well, I got a slap across my face. He hit me, I fall out of control. My girlfriend said, 'Marcus is not a hitting per-son, he just doesn't want you baby-sitting, maybe he wants you to depend on him.' I wasn't going for it. I wasn't going for any man hitting me, especially in my face. So I told him I did not want to see him again. I started receiving threats from him. Finally it just wound down, but I always knew that somewhere deep inside Marcus loved me.

"So then here comes the woman into my life.

"At that time, I used to wear my hair in a curly Afro. I used to ride bikes a lot, and I started being my little self, doing things that I liked. Guys didn't like me too much be-cause they thought I was a guy, they thought I acted more like a guy. To this day I get that kind of stuff, but I don't give a damn. Fuck what guys said, fuck them.

"My friend comes up to me and says, 'There's a friend of mine wants to meet you.' And I said, 'Who?' She tells me about this lady named Mabel.

"The reason why I'm smiling is 'cause that was my first experience with love, really. I had fallen in love again.

"My friend says, 'She wants you to come to her house and have dinner with her.' She walked up to me and says, 'Hi, I'm Mabel.' I said, 'Hi.' So I'm sitting there in this apartment with this woman. She's much older than me.

"I walked in her apartment, I sat down, we were having dinner, we were talking now. I was still kind of shy and I'm still naive, so I just do my own thing. I'm eating and she's talking to me and I'm eating and she shows me around. And in a little while, she's touching me in certain ways, touching me and going stroking my face and arms. It feels very strange, feels very strange the way she's touching me. I'm not familiar with those feelings. First of all, I'm not familiar with any feelings of real warm, caressy, touching. My mother hardly ever touched us, she barely ever stroked us, she barely ever hugged us, she rarely held us. My father neither too.

"All this stuff, I feel I'm being stimulated a lot and I don't know how to handle it. Plus I'm shy and I don't know what to say. I'm feeling very uncomfortable, so I started to say, 'I think I better go home.'

"She says, 'Nora, you don't have to go.' By this time it's the evening. She looks out the window and says, 'It's kind of late, it is kind of late and it's dark and I really don't want you going back home.' I lived in Harlem, and she lived way on the East Side of 135th Street. She said, 'I don't want you going home this late.'

"I'm saying, 'Well, you think, you think . . . ' Now mind you now, I can't make my own decisions, it's hard for me to say no, it's hard for me to say, 'No, I think I should go home.' It's hard because I'm shy, I'm rigid, I'm scared. So I agree with her, 'Maybe, maybe you're right, maybe I should stay the night,' not knowing what's about to happen.

"After dinner we sit down at the couch and watch TV. She's touching me, and she's holding me. Still on the couch and she's reading the paper, and she says, 'You okay?' She's stroking me like this and she's reading the *New York Times* and I'm watching TV. She says, 'Would you like anything else?' And she looks at the clock and it's getting on nine and she says, 'You know, I have to get up in the morning, so I think it's best we get ready, go to bed.' Then she gives me pajamas to put on and tells me where the shower is. I go take a shower and put my pajamas on and get in bed. We slept in her room. She had a nice place—big bed, giant bed, and a nice big heavy quilt. It was warm. I admired this lady 'cause one day I hope to be like her, have an apartment, nice things. It was very cozy and comfortable. I'm still afraid and shy but I felt comfortable with her, and safe, a little safe.

"Then we were in bed and she tells me to come over to her so she could try to put my head on her shoulder. So I don't answer. She's laying over there, taps me on the shoulder and says, 'Why don't you turn around and come over here?' I wonder, 'What the hell's going on?' Well, I never slept with my mother, so I thought, maybe this is what girls do, you know. My mother never held me in her arms lying down like that, never. It sounds good, 'cause my mother never did it. But I was still apprehensive.

"Mabel says, 'Nora, I'm not gonna hurt you.' When I heard that, it made me feel a little more comfortable. Then I moved over, and I moved closer to her and put my head on her. She's stroking me. We finally fell asleep, fell asleep like that.

"In the middle of the night, she gets up, so I turn over and I'm sleeping. She comes back, gets back in bed. I started to feel this hand going into my pants.

"Now mind you, as she pulls me over to her I'm very confused about these feelings and I'm very confused about all this touching. It's also scaring me. But it also makes me feel wanted, loved, like someone loves me, like someone loves me enough where they could touch me.

"She's gentle, in her words and in her voice. So she moves

me closer to her and I turn away. I'm still nervous, I'm still afraid. She says, 'I'm not gonna hurt you.' By now this woman has a feeling that I am very scared, but she goes like she's gonna try me anyway. She goes with her hand in my pajamas, in my underwear. Then she says to me, 'Why don't you take these off?' By this time, 'What is going on here?' You know, I'm really, really scared.

"I moved away from her real quick. I moved away from her like this, *real* quick. I moved away from her real quick. This is when she knows she has to leave me alone because I'm too frightened. She turns my face like this to her and she sees the look in my eyes and she knows that I'm *scared* to death and I'm about to cry.

"She leaves me alone. She says, 'Okay, I'm gonna talk to you.' She pulls me closer to her and she holds me tight and she says, 'I don't know what happened to you in the past.' She starts talking to me about this. She says, 'I guarantee you're gonna feel very good.'

"All of this talk she's telling me, God, man, nobody ever talked to me like that. My feelings are starting to get there, the more I go along, and *that* scared me. She doesn't touch me that night. The next night she did! She was determined not to let me get away!

"The second day, I'm watching TV, she comes home from work, and her routine is reading the newspaper. She's home reading the *New York Times,* and we had dinner, watched TV. After the show was over, we took a shower together and after the shower we sat on the couch.

"We went to bed and we continued to talk. Most of the time she's talking to me 'cause I'm still kind of shy. But all the while, I'm beginning to like her because I'm beginning to feel she's very loving and something my mother had never had and my father never had with me. I'm beginning to feel curious.

"We got into bed, and this time she didn't wait 'til I'm asleep. She started holding me, started caressing me, she started kissing me. Then something bold came out of me. She came over to me and she started kissing me and we had never tongue kissed up until this point.

"I was curious. I never thought I had this boldness in me. But I turned to her and I said, 'Why don't you kiss me right.' You know, like that. A shy person, a shy person. I thought I was shy, 'Why don't you kiss me right.' I don't know where that voice came from.

"Her lips were so soft like pillows, like silky pillows. When you touch it, it's so silky and fluffy, you know, like wow.

"I started to feel so excited. We were kissing, she was kissing and caressing me, and we had sex—she had sex rather. She had oral sex with me. But then down the line, she wouldn't let me have sex with her. She didn't say why. She never told me. I thought two people are supposed to share lovemaking, but I guess in the gay community at times you want one person to be passive and she's the more dominant partner, aggressive. From the little experience I have in the gay community, that's how I understand it. I guess that's what she meant, but then I didn't understand it at all. It hurt me a little bit, because she didn't explain it.

"The sex part was confusing to me, and scary. It was still scary 'cause I didn't allow her to go on and on and on and on. You know how they do the lovemaking on TV or in the movies—it's on and on and on and on—uptown and all around, uptown, standing up, underneath, over.

"I just had—I still had fears about sex.

"After that day, I stayed a third day because I was beginning to like this, you know. But I want to tell you something. It wasn't so much about the sex. It was more so with the affection I was getting. The affection to me was more, because it really made me feel so damn good. You know what it is to have somebody touch you and stroke you and caress you and hold you and talk to you in a soft voice, you know, when you never had that, never, never? Oh, man, that's the best feelings in the world. Man, that is something. More stimulating, more exciting than the sexual part."

IF THERE WERE a continuum along which Woodhouse women's conformity to dominant gender beliefs were ranged, Nora might lie at one end, while Crystal would be placed somewhere near the other. Crystal firmly believes in society's precepts for proper female roles, attributes, and concerns, though she seems refreshingly more liberated from Victorian sensibilities about sex than most Americans. For Crystal, affection may be nice, but she especially likes "the sexual part." Matter-of-factly, Crystal says, "I'm a woman that loves a lot of it."

Perhaps more than any other Woodhouse woman, Crystal is the height of conventional femininity. Always perfectly coifed, perfumed, and jeweled, Crystal "wants to look good for some man." In fact, she wishes she hadn't heard that douching is bad for you, since she likes how it makes her feel. "They got nice ones out, like musk, they got the musk ones," Crystal informs me. "I see ones that I do want to use," Crystal continues, "but I went to a clinic and they said douching could give more infections or something." On this issue, it seems Crystal is swayed more by clinicians than by advertisers. "I used to do it, then I stopped. I don't use because I don't know if it's good for me."

Crystal is just finishing up at the receptionist's desk when Nora and I get back from the supermarket. Walking with us to the library, Crystal proudly shows me her "list of things to do" which she wrote in between answering phones:

Davey Sullivan
Age = 4½
Shoe Size = 11½
Pants Size = 4–5
Shirt Size = 6

Organize
1. Fold my Clothes Better
  & Make Them Look Neater
2. Need one more Shelf
3.
4.

Accomplishments
1. Invest in more Jewelry

Need Plenty of Toys, Books,
Coloring Books & Crayons

Things to Invest In

1. *Color Television*
2. *Stereo System*
3. *A Wedding Gift for Raymond*
4. *Name Necklace*
5. *Name Bracelet*
6. *Name Ring*

7. *A Camera*
8. *A Walk-Man Copy*
9. *Fix one more necklace*
  & Buy a new one
10. *Get Braids for my Hair**
11. *Do Long Nails**
12. *Buy More New Perfumes****
13. Fix one Watch Band it's
  Very Important
14. *Purchase one more*
  PocketBook
15. *Clothes for Both Bryan*
  and Davey.

1. Make one copy of my House
  Keys
2. Design my own Wedding Dress
3. Find out when I'm going to get
  A Divorce from Gregory Howard

Look for new Hats for the
Winter

Need

Bars of Soap, Sexier
  Underwear & BRA'S
Hair Products, Hair Gel,
Toothpaste,
Deodorant

1. Buy a new key chain
1. I enjoy wearing different
  Make-up
  Foundation
  Blush
  Lipstick-Peach
  Eyeshadow

We turn to the cooking business at hand. Crystal notices Nora's white T-shirt with bold black lettering, "Women Make the Rules."

"I don't think that's fair," exclaims Crystal. "It should be equal. It's unfair if women make all the rules. I mean that's how it is with me and Raymond. It's equal."

Crystal has a handful of special interests: her fiance, Raymond; her children, Davey and Bryan; her father, who has died recently; and the special day programs she attends religiously.

"Have you seen the kids lately?" I ask Crystal.

Crystal gets up to get me the latest photos of her two boys. "Davey, my baby, he's the love of my life," she says. Whenever Crystal talks about the children, she giggles steadily but her eyes darken. "I'm sad," she tells me. On the last visit, the little boy clung to his father the whole time. "He doesn't love me anymore," Crystal mourns, "he only loves his father."

Also, she and Raymond have been having some problems lately, and Crystal doesn't know if she can trust him any more.

"My fiance"–Crystal always refers to Raymond like that–"he was stealing from me. I was very hurt when I found out that he was the one that was stealing my money." The way Crystal tells the story, Raymond tries to make her feel responsible for his stealing.

"He told me that I was so freely–like when I go to his house I would just go like that, put my things on the table, you know, I would take off my coat, take off my shoes. I was freely when I went to his house and he seen that and he thought I was the one who had a lot of money and I didn't, but he stole it."

"I couldn't even believe that he would do it," Crystal says, trying to decide if she will forgive him or not, go back with him or not. "I didn't want to believe," she continues, "but then again, he was making me feel like I was the one making up stories—you know, he was trying to make me go crazy—that was his way of dealing with the money that he stole from me. He apologized to me. Last year, he stole from me too. He admitted that he stole from me."

The situation is all the harder because Crystal has dreams, and most of them include Raymond. "I've been with Raymond for four years. And I was telling Raymond this morning, you know, I told him that the situations that I've been in, it would be very hard for me to ever go back to him. And then he calls me today, says he's gonna have a little job and he's gonna make a lot of money.

"I'm so anxious to be married to him. You want me to tell you about that? I used to have like a Marquis diamond— it looked like a Marquis, very expensive diamond. And one day we had a fight and an argument and I threw it back to him."

Crystal's love is pure. She loves him without money. She loves him without a job. He's "disabled," but she loves him anyway. He dabbles in drugs, but she stands by his side. The stealing, that's another story. She can barely tolerate the stealing. "I would love to be married to Raymond. I really love Raymond—not because he got money, or he's gonna get a job and he's gonna start making plans."

The couple met at a day treatment program, a place where there are activities for people with disabilities. Crystal describes Raymond's disability:

"He's been burned 100 percent. Some kids were playing with matches on a bus and he caught on fire and he's been disabled. He's had skin grafts all over his body. He's burned all over his arm, underneath his pit. He's got meat hanging down underneath his arm, and his butt and his back. At first, you know, I took it hard because I used to have to shower with Raymond. I thought that I would have to be one of the girls that would leave him, you know, 'cause there were a couple of girls that was in his life and they left him. But I stayed with him for four years. I had a lot of male friends and my life slowed down ever since I met Raymond. I never– I didn't even have a desire to be with another man. I tease him. When he calls I say, 'Yeah, I'm going to go meet a white man.'" Crystal lights up when she talks about Raymond, flirting with him and having fun.

Every time they have a date Crystal makes sure her hair is done up just right–maybe in cornbraids with extensions or her natural curl poufed up a bit. Their dates are always at Raymond's place. Crystal never leaves for a date before adding a touch of lipstick, some mascara, and blush.

Crystal explains why she generally goes to him rather than the other way around. "He has his own apartment. He lives with two other roommates in the Bronx. The majority of times I go over there and spend my time over there. He can't sleep here, but I can definitely go there." Referring to Woodhouse staff, Crystal says, "What can they say to me. I've been with him for four years. What are they going to say, 'Crystal, you can't stay there?' I wish they would come and tell me that, ha." Crystal wouldn't dream of having Raymond stay over, following Woodhouse's unwritten rule about visitors to the rooms.

Crystal gets back to the issue at hand. "I don't want to break up. Sometimes these problems come up to me and I don't know how to handle the situation. I told him about two, three hours ago. I said, 'We're not getting back Raymond, we're not never. I want all my clothes and I want our relationship to be over. It was only a couple of dollars, but those couple of dollars, they add up because I'm in the work program here and it adds up."

You can almost hear Crystal's wheels spinning. What's

a couple of dollars compared to loyalty and devotion? She starts to recall the time she was sick, and Raymond was there for her. "I was urinating on myself and when I got my menstruation, I saw so many clots of blood on my thighs. I was going through a lot of changes, and I was scared. I didn't know who to talk to. But Raymond stood by me, you understand. He stood by me. He always cares about me. Every time I have a problem, the man stays by me. And he says he doesn't want to break up with me. So now I hear that he's going through problems, and it's like why should I leave him?"

Besides, the single life isn't really for Crystal. Most of her relationships have been long term. There have been three important ones. Now in her early thirties, Crystal says, "I've been with Gregory for ten years, I've been with Reggie for four years, and I've been with Raymond for four years." In fact, Crystal is still legally married to Gregory, the father of her eight-year-old son, Bryan.

Crystal explains what went wrong with her marriage. "When I got married I was still living in my mother's house, and that's why me and Gregory's relationship never worked out, at least that's what I think. I lived there and me and him never had our own apartment. Living in my mother's house didn't give us a chance to grow up, you know, and raise Bryan, 'cause I was pregnant with Bryan. I think it didn't give me a chance to be a woman. I mean, does that make sense? If I was living with Gregory, if we had our own apartment, I think I would have grown up with him, learned some responsibility, and I think I would've probably still been married to him.

"I think my depression started when my marriage was on the rocks. Me and Gregory was breaking up. He was such a fine guy, you know. I love his head. I loved everything about him. We was together for so long, you know. I guess, I think that's when my problems probably started."

Crystal looks a little down thinking about the pending divorce from Gregory. Crystal wants the divorce, especially since it will free her to marry Raymond. Still, she can't help feeling sorry. "Me and Gregory's breaking up," Crystal repeats as if to remind herself. "He was such a fine guy, you know. I love his head, I loved everything about him. We was together for so long, you know." Even if he did beat her, on occasion.

Crystal is terribly disappointed that she is unable to make a baby for her fiance. She wishes she could have another baby, but she'd first have to have her "tubes untied." Crystal doesn't think having the procedure to reverse the tubal ligation is a realistic option. "They tell me that it would cost thousands and thousands of dollars. First of all, after they untie my tubes, it's not a sure thing that I would be able to produce children. They say it may not work out. And if I was to have another baby, I might have another cesarean and complications. I get depressed, I get depressed about that. You know, wanting to have another child, can't have one."

At least there's no need to use contraceptives, Crystal notes–the good part about having had the tubal ligation. Still, it wasn't her idea to have the procedure done. "I really didn't want it. I did it 'cause my mother and a lot of other caseworkers were around me. And they strapped my arms down and they gave me an injection in my left arm, I guess. Then I went to sleep. And I know that I was shaved down there, completely."

Now, Crystal wishes she could give to Raymond what she has already presented to the two other important men in her life. "The reason I think I want to have another baby is because Raymond, he doesn't have any children. I'll tell you, I wish that I could do it again. I wish that I could have another kid. And it would be Raymond's, you know. What I liked most about being pregnant was I could see my stomach growing everyday. And I had fun trying to push them out, but it didn't work out like that. Davey, I was almost losing him because he wasn't going through my cervix, and I was already 250 pounds. So they had to do an emergency C–section on me. I had a c-section on the first one too. They gave me stitches, I think like twenty-four stitches.

"I want there to be another one, but a lot of people–my mother, my caseworker, and, you know, Raymond's sick and I'm not all that together. And to bring a baby into the world.

"And the fact that I took an HIV test and I spoke with one of the workers there–"

"Oh," I interrupt, "What were the results of the test?"

"Good," Crystal answers, "Positive, that means good, right? I really don't know positive or negative, I forgot. I know that I don't have HIV. I don't have it."

Following the American dream, Crystal just wants a husband, her children, and the means to purchase the goods she itemized on her shopping list. No one else seems to be holding up their side of the deal–Crystal says she is stopped at all turns by family and professionals who say they know what's best for her. She wants to marry Raymond on the patio at Woodhouse. So far, they haven't set a date because everyone around them thinks they shouldn't do it. The couple has already put off the wedding several times.

"I was going to get married about four times to Raymond," Crystal explains. "The therapists monitor us and they say, 'Oh, you're not ready for marriage, you're not ready.' And I said okay. Then my father and my mother used to say, 'Oh, you're not ready to get married, you're not ready to get married.' And I said okay. And my caseworker said, 'Oh, you're not ready to get married, you still got too many problems, you can't handle marriage.' I said okay. Now the fourth time, my father died and they really told me, 'You're not ready for marriage, you're not going to be able to cope

with marriage.' Again. You know. So I heard so many voices,
I heard a lot of people's voices. So I just listened to them.

"Right now, if Raymond could get better, I think maybe
we can get married. If he could work on his illness, I mean.
He has a problem, a problem with stealing."

IT'S BEEN YEARS since some of the women have had a
relationship with a man. For Diane, it's been fourteen years,
Hattie, nearly fifteen, Sol Revilla, nine, Denise, five, and
Dixie, about three.

While living in a downtown shelter, Sarah turned down
several invitations for dates. Ever since her husband died,
Sarah has had no interest in other men. Lately, she's had
a change of heart. "I'm beginning to feel lonely," Sarah
explains.

Many years have passed since Dixie was a bride. Unlike
Crystal, Dixie as a newlywed insisted to her new husband
that they set up housekeeping on their own. This was when
Dixie was twenty-one years old, living in New Jersey, and
working as a nurse's aide in the emergency room of a local
hospital.

One day, a strong, handsome guy strolled through the
emergency room. The fellow had a laceration on his finger,
a work-related injury. The whole while he was being ban-
daged up, he and Dixie talked and talked and talked. Paul
told Dixie he was twenty-four years old and asked her out
on a date.

Over time, the couple began getting very close. Dixie remembers the time Paul's mother called her to join the family
for a surprise birthday party for her son. It turned out to be a
special birthday—Paul's eighteenth! Dixie was shocked and
Paul was angry, his secret now out.

The age difference didn't matter after all, and the couple was married two years later. At first, they really struggled. Dixie recalls how difficult it was for Paul to separate from his family, but the new wife put her foot down. She absolutely refused to move in with his parents, insisting they make it on their own.

The young couple had no money, and the early years were difficult. Paul was apprenticing to become an electrician. Dixie found work close to home cleaning houses for wealthy New Jersey families.

It's not that the family didn't help out. They were very good about that, Dixie recalls, and did for them in ways respectful of the new couple's pride. "Sometimes," Dixie recounts by way of example, "we'd eat dinner at his mother's house and she'd pack up some food in Tupperware for us to take home. It made a difference."

Once Paul was accepted to the electrician's union, their financial situation improved. Dixie quit her day jobs and stayed home. The couple didn't have children. Dixie says, "It just never came up, it wasn't an issue." In the nearly twelve years they were married, Dixie says, "We didn't try to have children, we also didn't try not to. It never happened, so I guess it just wasn't in the cards."

The divorce came after Paul started fooling around with other women. A good lawyer helped Dixie get half the value of the house. Dixie's ex has a new family now—a wife and a couple of kids. He still lives in the house.

The last time Dixie got involved was before she moved into Woodhouse. The fellow's name was Artie, and he was her boyfriend for eight years. Artie earned a living as a windshield washer. "He actually made a good amount of money," she assures me, "It helped support us, brought in about thirty dollars a day."

The problem with Artie was his alcoholism. Dixie says,

"When he was drinking, he was great and had a great personality." Then he would sober up, becoming "mean and horrible." Dixie wonders if he was "craving alcohol or going through withdrawal." All she knows is "he was horrible, he abused me, beat me." One day, Artie proposed marriage.

"Marry an alcoholic? Just what I need," Dixie says she told him. In fact, when the hitting started, Dixie walked out on him altogether. "Neither of my husbands ever hit me," Dixie says with pride. She certainly wasn't going to let this guy start on her. "I'd read about these abusive husbands in magazines," Dixie goes on, "I could never understand why these women didn't just leave them."

Dixie chuckles. "A funny thing. When I started going out with Carl, I really missed my husband Paul." With Artie in the picture, Dixie found herself longing for Carl.

These days, Dixie has no desire to date. She no longer yearns for any man.

Dominique has been unusually quiet throughout the conversation.

She's been thinking about her old fiance, Anthony. Even though she broke up with him, it doesn't mean she's forgotten about him. Even though he started chasing other Woodhouse women, it doesn't mean she's lost all feeling for him.

"Why did you break up?" I ask.

"He started bribin' me," Dominique begins her tale. "He'd take me shopping if I'd come to his apartment and have sex with him."

"I didn't like the bribe so I broke up with him," she says. "I never did have sex with him," she states in front of the crowd at the table.

"What are you saying?" Nora doesn't hide her disbelief. "You told me you had sex with him."

Dominique smiles coyly, then "admits" to the sex.

"At first," she tells us, "he didn't take me shopping. But then he started taking me shopping.

"Sometimes, I'd go to his apartment with him. Sometimes I did and sometimes I didn't. Then he started saying, 'If you want me to take you shopping, you have to come to my apartment after.' I didn't like this, but since I like to buy a lot of things . . ." Dominique stops to roll her eyes as if calculating how much sex she'd have to have with him to get all the goods on her shopping list.

"I broke it off with him," Dominique continues. "I told him he should find someone else. Then he told me he did like someone else, someone here at Woodhouse. Diane. Diane Williams.

"I told him next time he comes to Woodhouse, he should ask for Diane Williams, not Dominique Deveroe.

"Next time he came here, he asked for Diane Williams and for me. Neither one of us came down to see him."

Nora sympathizes. Anthony reminds her of this guy she kind of likes. "His name is Eddie. He's this cute little Spanish guy with one problem—he likes to tell me what to do." Nora supposes that, "since he's Spanish, he likes women to dress in skirts and stuff like that. I have a closet full of dresses, but I'm not gonna change what I wear 'cause he tells me to." On the other hand, Nora believes, "He likes me 'cause I'm like a challenge to him. We fist fight together."

Then he lied to her and Nora can't take that. "Even though he's so cute," she says, "he lied to me, hurt me, and I don't trust him."

"Oh," Hattie sighs, "I'd like a man who is normal, not like me. You know, someone who has never had a nervous breakdown. Someone who hasn't been on Haldol and hasn't gone off the deep end."

7

Odd Women Out

THE MENU FOR the day is hamburgers with fries, and a salad. Sharlea is the head chef. As is her style, Sharlea slowly and deliberately works the meat patties, careful to protect her inch-long fingernails polished, this time, in lavender. Dixie prepares the salad, while I peel and cut up potatoes.

"You know my aunts who raised me after my parents died? I don't know if it was the talk we had or what," Dixie says of our recent conversations, "but I sent them a letter. I wrote a letter to my two maiden aunts on my father's side. I haven't seen them in about ten years and I decided to write. I thought maybe they'll get in touch with me, we'll see. I thought, we'll see, I'm not putting my hopes up. If they do, they do.

"They did. They got in touch with me. They came to visit me last Tuesday. I was nervous, it had been ten years.

"They stayed three and a half hours. They brought me some chocolates and a plaque that says, 'You are Loved.' They said it was for my birthday. They remembered my birthday."

Felice Mills peers into the library. She doesn't want to join us. "I'm keeping to myself," she tells us. "Since everyone

127

leaves all the time, I'm not gonna get involved with anybody, and I'm not gonna talk to anybody either." It's been several weeks since Felice's case manager left for vacation.

Margery is helping with the potatoes but not doing a very good job. Felice tells her so, and Margery gladly hands her the potato.

Felice, peeling feverishly, begins to talk. "I had one child, a daughter. But she's dead, and so is my grandson. They died in a car accident. My daughter was twenty-seven years old and the boy was four.

"My husband died in the same crash. It was on the New Jersey Turnpike. My husband, he brought them into the world and then he took them away.

"I don't want to have anything more to do with people. I decided then I hate people." Then, in barely her next breath, Felice says, "I like your bracelets. Can I have them?"

"I'm sorry," I answer, "these were a gift from my husband. I can't give them away."

"Okay," Felice goes on, "But there's a place that sells beautiful Indian bracelets up the street."

Switching topics, Felice continues, "Since I'm schizophrenic, when I get angry and upset I tear my own clothes off my body."

All this while, Felice is scraping potatoes. Suddenly she stops, drops the potato and peeler on the table. "Every time I cook I start talking about my private business. Every time I start cooking. I'm not going to cook no more."

She turns away from the table, picks a book off the library shelf, and announces its title, *Odd Woman Out*. "This is me," she says, "I'm an odd woman, so I should probably get out."

"I don't think you're odd," I say. "I like your company, and I hope you'll stay."

"Ha," she snaps back, "you like me because you're odd too, and odd people like odd people."

IN THE MONTHS to come, stealing at Woodhouse gets bad and rumor has it that Felice is the main culprit. Some women report seeing her with their possessions. Also, her affair with crack seems to be getting more intense. Staff offer to help her move into a therapeutic community, if that's what she wants.

This night it is only a small group for dinner. Nora sweeps the floor under the table where we work, muttering, "This is filthy. I can't cook and I can't eat in a place like this." I agree. I find the dirty stove, greasy counters, and lack of supplies in the kitchen area disheartening. One of these days, I think to myself, I'll come in just to do a thorough cleaning.

For now, I want to know what people think of Woodhouse.

"This place is blessed, and this place is a blessing," Nora assures me. Denise says the best thing about Woodhouse is it "changed my life from homeless to having a home." "It's paradise," agrees Teri, who especially appreciates getting "help when you need it" from Woodhouse staff. Teri almost shudders at the notion of having a place of her very own, because "if I needed help or was in a crisis, I might not be able to get the help I would need." In an apartment, she imagines herself in crisis and alone.

Not everyone feels about Woodhouse the way Nora, Denise, and Teri do. For Sarah, the best thing about Woodhouse is "not worrying where you're going to stay," and the worst thing is that "if you get a job, you won't realize anything because you will lose your SSI benefits, so you have to earn more than your SSI." Sarah says, "I still want to tackle it, but it's self-defeating."

Sarah also dreams of having her own place some day, because "I like to cook for myself and miss the chance to do so." She also believes that she would prepare better, healthier food for herself than she eats at the Woodhouse cafeteria. "The cafeteria food is fattening," Sarah says. "It's heavy and there's a lot of bread, rice, potatoes, gravy, and spaghetti. Breakfast, for example, might be pancakes with heavy syrup and sausages, followed by lunch of chili on rice. The snacks are all sugary stuff–candy bars, cakes. If I prepared my own foods, I would prepare boiled potatoes with margarine and a green salad. When I had my own place, my meat intake would be two pounds of hamburger meat a week–I'd pre-pare a meat loaf and eat it over a period of a week. You can watch it better when you are cooking for yourself. With the kinds of food at Woodhouse, your body will put on the weight. It's not good for your self-esteem to be constantly battling your weight."

Diane, who especially likes "my room and watching my TV," said, "I'd like to make my own food, I'd like that." Smithy agrees; in fact, she's planning to move out of Woodhouse to a residence in the Bronx where "I will be able to prepare my own food in a kitchen on the floor and have my own room."

"The way they prepare food is just awful," says Dixie. "They always bake everything–baked ham, baked lamb chops, baked steak–what's that? I may be crazy but I still know how to cook!" Dixie went on, "Baked steak–who bakes steak? A steak is supposed to be broiled!"

Sarah says she tries not to let it upset her, but she really wants to get out and live in her own apartment. Still, she is quick to point out the little things staff members at Wood-house do for residents. Victoria Leyton, Woodhouse's clini-cal director, arranges several bouquets of flowers for the cafeteria tables each year on Mother's Day. Nick, one of the cooks, prepared a delicious roast beef dinner. For holi-days, Nick and Lenore, another house chef, prepare special things, like avocado dip with chips and blueberry cake. For St. Patrick's Day, Lenore prepared a turkey with all the trim-

mings. Sarah says, "They hire people who get joy out of
doing special things for people—it makes you feel like somebody cares."

There are bound to be problems when fifty people live together and see each other every day for breakfast, lunch,
and dinner. "The women get on each other's nerves," notes
Diane. "Some of the women get into nonsense, wishy-washy
attitudes and arguing."

Dixie explains it like this: "The biggest problem is I have
to see, talk to, be around other women all the time. Sometimes I just want to be alone, completely alone, and there's
no place for me to do that except when I'm in my room.
Sometimes I don't want to be in my room like that. I want
to be in the dining room, not in my bedroom, but in your
kitchen, at the table with a cup of coffee. At Woodhouse,
you always have to see the other women and it gets on my
nerves."

"I'm sure I get on the nerves of the other women too,"
Dixie continues, "it's just the situation."

MORE THAN half of the women who live at Woodhouse
have been here since the first year it opened. Many others
move in and out over the course of a year. Sometimes, a
woman may become too sick or disabled to maintain the
relatively independent life-style assumed at Woodhouse. At
that point, the directors may decide the best course of action
is a move to a nursing home or psychiatric hospital, depending on the situation. It is not always easy for staff to find
the proper placement for those who have become incapaci-
tated, especially in these days of ever-growing austerity in
health care.

Staff have been known to use the best of their skill and
strategy in confronting the health care bureaucracy on be-

half of clients. I have witnessed them beg, plead, cajole, and raise their voices to secure temporary or permanent placement for those women who can no longer manage the "activities of daily living" at Woodhouse. At times, staff go beyond the call of duty to provide care for desperate women. For example, case manager Clare became physically and emotionally exhausted after months of grooming, wiping, moving, and cleaning Willetta Hull, an elderly and incontinent woman no longer able to do the simplest thing for herself. As Victoria struggled to find placement in a nursing home, Clare continued to care for Willetta throughout each day, in addition to fulfilling her other duties as a Woodhouse case manager.

For the woman who may need extra care, news that she will be moved to another facility is often unwelcome. Like Willetta, Estella Leonard, a diabetic with a drinking problem, became unable to care for herself and was placed in a nursing home. After several weeks there, Estella wandered away and came back to Woodhouse. Susan doesn't think the staff had any choice but to send Estella back to the nursing home.

"This is a therapeutic setting," Susan explains. "We're all on medication, and if we get to the point where we can't take care of ourselves, then they have to put us someplace else."

Nora empathizes with Estella and argues with Susan, "Estella's really angry 'cause they put her in this place she doesn't want to be in, and who knows what'll happen to her belongings left here. And what about her cat? Gary [a case manager] said he'd take it, but he's leaving for vacation soon, and then what'll happen to her cat? The way Estella sees it, they didn't do what is best for her, but they did something *to* her—that's how it feels to Estella."

Susan still disagrees. "Even though this is our home and we pay rent, Estella was way out of control. She was out of control with her drinking and out of control with her diarrhea. You go in the bathroom, there's diarrhea on the floor, all over the toilet, on the sink. She walks around with diarrhea on her clothes, on her hands. It's on the steps."

Nora still disagrees. "Estella's not happy. She came back home. They sent her away again and she resents it."

Other women who become too "disruptive" are asked to move out, only to once again live on the street or in a city shelter. Women with a taste for alcohol or drugs are often the biggest trouble makers, especially those unable or unwilling to admit they have a problem. At Woodhouse, eviction usually comes after one too many infractions, usually hassling other women for money or simply stealing it.

At first, I am not surprised by these departures. Later, each new eviction comes as a shock—Sonia Morales, Felice Mills, Alma Garrison, Debra Brown would eventually be evicted. Most times, the women hear about these moves through the grapevine, not in an official way, which leaves many thinking, "Am I next?" The topic was even addressed by the women who participate in their monthly tenants meeting, though the question, "Can they evict people as easily as they do—just like that?" was left unanswered.

The women seem to follow an unwritten rule about visitors to their rooms. While they may receive guests in their rooms, most of the women say men are unwelcome upstairs. On occasion, there are exceptions. Joseph and his fiancée, Patsy, sometimes spend time in her room, though he has never spent the night.

Many women seem to like it that way. They don't want men—strange men, familiar men—in the corridors, near their rooms. After all, the showers are down the hall. Imagine having to get dressed every time you need to use the toilet. Besides, safety and security is important too. Too many Woodhouse women have had their fill of fending off advances and assaults from men they did not want. Who needs to worry about that here? Of course, it would be nice to have your regular guy in your own place. You could fix him a little snack, maybe crackers and cheese and some fruit. "It makes me feel like a three year old," Nora once remarked on the rule. "It's like going to Mommy for permission," she said about having to get clearance from the directors before you have a visitor upstairs.

Even with restrictions on visitors, "things walk out of here," Diane says, "Stealing is a big problem around here." Sarah reports the theft of her wallet. It happened on a particularly hot night when Sarah decided to keep her door open to sleep more comfortably. Someone crept into her room and walked away with her wallet. "It had my California driver's license, some credit cards, and eleven dollars," Sarah says. "Eleven dollars isn't much, but it's something."

Susan is still upset about the theft of her VCR two years ago, when she had just moved into Woodhouse. She traces most thefts to Woodhouse's loose policy with the master key. "The guards give out the master key too easily," Susan points out. "All someone has to do is make an impression of the key in some wax and get a key made." Susan says she requested and was granted a lock for her room that can't be opened by the master key. "Felice is another one who steals," Susan tells me. "One time she walked into Dominique's room when Dominique was there and Felice hadn't realized Dominique was in there."

"The problem is," concludes Susan, "there's not enough supervision by staff of some of the residents."

"Like who?" I wanted to know.

"Dominique, for one." It seems that Dominique is known for unusual displays at odd moments. During dinner she might decide to drape her three-hundred-pound-plus body across several chairs. Or she might start to sing, out of the blue. "Dominique's singing isn't like normal singing," explains Susan. "It's just these loud sounds, but Dominique *thinks* she's singing." Dominique's also known for knocking on some people's doors in the middle of the night, pounding on the door, demanding a cigarette.

"Who else?" I ask.

"Alma, because she's always outside panhandling and doing drugs. Denise, because she's drinking too much. Debra, because she's a crackhead. And Willetta Hull, because she's always peeing all over the place."

AUGUST IS a particularly tough time at Woodhouse. While a handful of residents may be away visiting family or friends, it's mostly the staff who take their vacation time then.

One August day, all I do is walk into the building to sense that things are generally falling apart. Some kind of chaos hangs in the air. So many people hanging around. It's another very hot day in New York—we've been having ninety-degree-plus days, and the heat just doesn't seem to want to break.

There is air conditioning in the dayroom and in the cafeteria. Some women have fans in their rooms, but fans don't help on oppressively hot days. For the women who live in the middle of the building—the shaftway—it is impossible to breathe. No air circulates in the middle rooms. Those women have to hang out downstairs until the sun goes down.

Victoria says the past week had been particularly bad. "Everybody's decompensating and incontinent," she says in frustration. "They've been peeing all over the place, and it's been a terrible week."

This year promises to be no different than every other. Gary, a case manager, is gone for the month, and Victoria has had to take a lot of time off to care for a sick relative. Another case manager, Patricia, just up and left altogether, without even saying good-bye to the women who make up her caseload. She took her two weeks vacation time and never came back.

Jill broke the news to the clients in her caseload that she'll be leaving to start school in September. That means there will be two new case managers–one to replace Patricia and one for Jill.

Toby Sands and Janice Wilson no longer live at Woodhouse. They had become too "disruptive" and the administration arranged for them to move out.

And old Madeline Miller died in August too.

In September, Vera, the new case manager hired to replace Patricia, started on the job. The place is buzzing about her style and personality. The first time I see Vera she is arguing with Crystal in the hallway. I make my way past them to find Susan and Hattie in the library.

"She's not at all like Jill," Susan points out. "From the very first, Jill was so warm and open."

Hattie agrees, "Vera has a heart like an ice cube." She feels Vera treats her "like a criminal, like a stone-cold killer." Hattie describes Vera. "She has a big broad smile with lots of white teeth, but her eyes are cold and she won't look at you when you speak."

At Woodhouse, clients and case managers have private meetings on a regular basis. A few days ago, it was Hattie's turn to meet with Vera. "I sat through the meeting looking down at my lap," Hattie reports. "I couldn't look at her, the way she makes me feel. She's a cold fish," Hattie concludes.

In the next breath, Hattie urges compassion for the new worker. "Vera's nervous because she's new, so she's acting strict and cold, and maybe she's afraid we women will take advantage of her." Hattie hopes Vera's clients will understand this, "give her a chance, and maybe she'll loosen up after a while." Still, Hattie wonders, "When will Vera get accustomed to her job and start getting relaxed and at ease. She's making me and everyone else nervous."

Hattie is particularly upset with the way Vera is handling room inspections. Hattie is one of Woodhouse's model residents. In fact, her room has been described as "a showcase." Nevertheless, everyone has to have their room inspected by their case manager, even Hattie. According to Hattie, Jill always showed respect, only checking her room once every six months. And in the interim between "inspections," Jill would never forget to ask Hattie if she needed anything for her room.

Now, Vera has informed Hattie her room will be inspected weekly. "This is demeaning," Hattie complains. "I always keep my room in order. Why should my room be inspected because some other people are slobs and live in a pigsty?"

These weekly inspections are a new policy, or a revision of an old policy, at Woodhouse. Hattie is outraged. Some say the reason they are inspecting everyone's room is so that no particular resident feels singled out. To that, Hattie says, "It's unfair. Why are the feelings of the person who's a slob count more than those of the person who is neat?" Some say the weekly inspections come out of a concern for fire and safety issues. To that, Hattie says, "This is the first step in the direction of more inspections. The next thing you know, they're going to look in our laundry, our bags, and things like that."

Hattie has already gone above her case manager to see if she can straighten things out. She'll be meeting with Vera again tomorrow. "I'm going to tell her when she can, when she can't inspect my room," Hattie plans. She is pessimistic about how the meeting will go. "I've already asked Vera if I could have my room inspected once a month, not once a week. She's already said no. She said, 'It's a directive and I'm following orders.'"

Vera has been having the same problem with her other clients. When I had seen them in the hallway, she and Crystal had been arguing about the state of Crystal's room. Vera thinks it's "too messy." Her threat rings in Crystal's head: "If you want your son to visit you at Woodhouse, you better do something about your room."

I see Crystal in the dining room and she invites me up to her room. The last time I had been there, it was a mess. Clothes were piled everywhere, stuffed in the closet, pouring out of the drawers. The room is in much better condition now. No clothes are on her bed, but piled in several large boxes along one wall. There seems to be no order to the piles.

"Do you need *all* these clothes?" I ask.

"Oh yes," Crystal explains, "I change my outfit three or four times a day."

"Hmm." I wonder what the solution might be. The room is only about twelve feet by twelve feet, enough for a bed, a night table, a chair, a dresser. "Do you really need every single one of these clothes?" I can't think of any better solution than to dispose of some. "Maybe you could sort through them and get rid of some things you don't really use. Can you get another dresser, or a bookshelf for the clothes in these boxes?"

Crystal starts to laugh. "There's more," she confesses, as she lifts a bed cover to reveal another batch of clothes piled under her bed. "It's my secret hiding place," she says.

BECAUSE SHE is short-staffed, Victoria asks if I will help out with the cooking group. I wonder if Dixie wants to work with me, but she is down in the dumps today. She had a run-in with one of two teenage girls hired for the summer. The two youth workers live in the neighborhood and were placed at Woodhouse through a special youth employment program. Both are fifteen years old, and their job is to assist case managers throughout the day. Charisse is the nice one. The other one's name is Lana.

Dixie is so upset, she has lapsed into a depression over the incident. Six days have already passed, and Dixie can't seem to shake it. In the quiet of nurse Eleanor's office, Dixie tells me what happened: "This girl, Lana, she comes into the cafeteria and she turned the TV to her channel soap opera–channel four. We don't watch channel 4 soap opera, first of all. She has no right coming in to turn the TV on to her channel. She just walked in and changed the channel. So then she left, after about twenty minutes. So then she left and I turned the channel to what we usually watch–to seven.

"She comes back yellin' and screamin', 'Who turned the TV? *Who* turned the TV?' Nobody said anything. '*Who* turned the TV, I said?'

"So I said, 'I did.'

"'Who do you think you are?' She's pointing her finger at me. 'You're supposed to ask permission before you touch that TV,' she said to me. 'You're not supposed to turn that channel, don't you touch that TV.' After that she went back into the office.

"I told [program director] Marvin, 'You better check out your student because I'm not gonna be spoken to in that respect.' But it was already too late. I became so depressed. A fifteen year old yelling at me in my own home, in my own house. Gary said that instead of feeling shitty, I should talk to Marvin about it. So I did speak to Marvin. He said she's got no right coming in turning the channel to her program, and no right yelling at me. To be rude, it made her feel important. I'm having such a strong reaction 'cause she's some fifteen-year-old little snot yelling at me that way in my own house. She thinks she's hot shit. I'm so depressed I don't feel like doing anything."

THE "ARROGATION of the right to define needs," Michael Ignatieff once wrote, is a "warrant for abuse." Ignatieff also submits that "there are few presumptions in human relations more dangerous than the idea that one knows what another human being needs better than they do themselves" (1985:11). Tactical power unleashed, staff at Woodhouse address the presumed needs of residents. Aside from all else, assumptions about their needs position Woodhouse women precariously. And the institution gets mixed reviews by the women who live there.

In the field of power relations at Woodhouse, power is passed through all its staff, from the top directors to the receptionist/guards, and the women know it. This is the "relative powerlessness of residents" in relation to staff that subjects Woodhouse women to potential mistreatment. This is what makes the women vulnerable to a case manager like Vera, who leaves respect at the door and, in the execution of her job, exercises undue authoritarianism. It also leaves them vulnerable to the kind of abusive exchange Dixie faced with the teenage worker. The women also know they are required to submit to a higher authority, whether in the form of room inspections or evictions.

At the same time, the women consider Woodhouse "a blessing" and "paradise." In part, this positive review derives from a comparison to places more dreadful than Woodhouse, like city shelters and the street. But it also derives from the experience of living in a setting guided by an explicitly nondirective philosophy under Victoria's lead: "The looser we are, the more it works." At Woodhouse there is some room within which residents may determine their own needs.

The nature of social relations at Woodhouse is shaped by the logic of its mandates and organizational structure. There is no avoiding the onus of Woodhouse's institutional imperative; nevertheless, subtle differences of philosophy and policy do affect quality of life. At least under Victoria's tenure, Woodhouse policies and philosophies have some positive implications: Vera is dismissed, the teenage worker is reprimanded and provided instruction on proper behavior, and Dresden successfully organized an in-house "community tenant's group."

Places like Woodhouse can respond only partly to the human needs at its doorstep. Constrained, as are the women themselves, by forces beyond its control, the institution and its representatives face contradictory demands and expectations. They cannot transform the larger social conditions that put people at risk for what besieges them. They also cannot escape a double-agent role: they are at once a system of healing and an instrument of surveillance. In a direct way, they "serve" the people in their charge; indirectly, they serve to maintain "the surplus" at a minimal standard of living and take "visible poverty" off the street.

Woodhouse is not responsible for effecting social change, but for maintaining and reproducing a population under existing social conditions. In fact, as programs are developed, root causes of social problems are neglected and generally dismissed as unsolvable. Nevertheless, the distorted political arguments of the day attack places like Woodhouse for not solving the greater social issues. Programs are often then deemed "ineffective," and funding is further threatened. As these programs struggle to survive, they must move even farther from the broader issues. Woodhouse is not alone in this predicament; virtually all social programs are mired in these dilemmas.

The contradictions are dizzying. Woodhouse women are at once vulnerable and strong, failures and survivors. They are at once in need of "help," "healing," and "teaching," a paternalistic and infantalizing approach, and at the same time they need respect, freedom and autonomy, independence. Woodhouse is at once a home that nurtures, heals, cares, embraces, and a precarious institution that names and labels, constructing otherness and essentializing women's experiences with poverty, homelessness, mental illness. Just as the women signify our social problems, Woodhouse is emblematic of our social solutions, always fragmented and partial.

8

Pistachio Nuts

I ARRIVE EARLY to set up the arroz con pollo I've prepared at home for today's cooking group. The work has been done ahead of time, leaving no chores for any of the women.

The enormous white pot attracts attention as I carry it through to the library. "It looks so good." "It smells so good." "When do we eat?" I am pleasantly bombarded with questions. "You did this for *us?*" someone shouts from the hallway.

"You must have a really nice kitchen," another remarks, carefully checking out the quality and quantity of food and tools I've brought in.

A group of women settles at the table. The library fills with the fragrance of onion and pepper *sofrito,* green olives and capers, garlic, *bijol,* and beer. While they wait, the women sit in a strange, passive silence.

Suddenly Hattie speaks up. "It's Sol," she tells me, "she's decompensating."

Before I can reply, Hattie says, "Well, anyway, that's what the case managers are saying. But what does 'decompensating' mean?"

"I'm not sure," I answer honestly.

"I think it means her medicine isn't working well anymore," Hattie surmises.

Sol is having accidents all the time now, urinating on herself. Sol always had this problem, but it's getting worse. She tries to use Depend but finds they really don't help when you have a full bladder. Depends are good for if you're on the bus or something and you let a little urine out, but it's not for when you have a full bladder.

When they see she is wet, Sol's friends remind her to change her clothes. It's so humiliating that Sol just gets mad at them.

Sol has been yelling at Hattie. "She says things like 'I hate white people,'" reports Hattie. "It's just that she is so angry because she knows she is peeing on herself and that ashames her and she doesn't have control over herself, and all of this makes her very angry. Something is happening with her medication."

Sol Revilla has no teeth and always wears a baseball cap. With a bright red tongue and bright red gums against her deep brown skin, Sol's coloring is remarkable. She looks at least twenty more than her forty-something years.

Sol never would meet with me for a formal, private chat. She explains, "Every time I talk to anyone, they never listen to me." Sometimes we would hang out outside the front door or in the dayroom.

Sol has spent her life in and out of institutions. She lists about fifteen different people all with the last name of Revilla who didn't visit her when she was in the hospital. She doesn't want to have anything to do with them anymore, ever again. These are people who call themselves family, but they had nothing to do with her when she was sick in the hospital and now her mother is dead. Sol is sucking her thumb and petting her head.

She has lived in five different Manhattan and Bronx hospitals. Eventually, she ran away from most of them. After the last runaway, Sol found herself in a shelter, and then she was brought to Woodhouse.

By then, her mother was dead. Sol can't believe her mother would leave her like that. She was kissing her mama when she died, stroking her head. She was dead. Her mother had false teeth, and Sol was worried she would choke on them. Sol removed the teeth from her mother's mouth. Her mother's lungs burst and the ambulance guys said they couldn't do anything for her. She was DOA, dead on arrival.

Sol loves Ronald Reagan and says she's always been a Republican. The Democrats are always taking away people's money. One day, Sol saw Ronald Reagan. She was just walking down the street when she saw him. He told her that when the three golden worms appear in front of her eyes, it was a sign that she, Sol Revilla, should go away. Sol wouldn't say where she was supposed to go to. Sol belly-laughs, "I'm not going to tell you *that* secret."

Sol likes Woodhouse because here they don't force you to go to programs. She's tired of programs. The smile on her face comes and goes. When it goes, Sol looks violently angry and her expression becomes sinister, almost murderous. Sol has a loud, piercing cackle that she lets out every once in a while—sometimes at me, sometimes at a person walking by in the street.

Sol has two kids. One is twelve, and one is nine. They live with relatives. One came from a man she was living with because she didn't have any other place to go.

Linda Williams is Sol's best friend. Linda is Sol's mother come down from the dead. Linda smiles and nods her head. Sol asks Linda, "Aren't you my mother? Aren't you my mommy?"

J UST THIS morning, Sol lifted her dress up in the dining room for everyone to see her panties. A little while later, she had an accident, wetting herself again. She took off her underpants, put them on her head, and lifted her skirt up again. Everyone quickly tried to look away. Hattie says, "I didn't turn away fast enough, and I did see Sol naked."

I need some salt from the main kitchen. On my way downstairs, I see Sol, who was wide-eyed and nearly incoherent. But she knows me and gives me a wet kiss hello. As is usual for her, Sol steps outside herself and asks after my children. She never forgets my daughter, who sometimes comes with me to Woodhouse. "How's Leah? Where's your little girl? Why isn't she here?" Sol asks.

HEADING TOWARD Woodhouse on Broadway one morning, I catch a glimpse of a familiar figure standing on the street corner, her hand outstretched for a dime or a quarter. It's Alma, a slip of a woman, who looks as if she's had one too many hits of crack this chilly spring morning. Alma's tongue flutters in and out of her dry mouth as her half-opened eyes do their best to plead for a couple of coins. I wonder if she will acknowledge me this time.

"Good morning Alma," I greet her as I pass by. No answer.

It's funny about Alma. She can attach herself to you or tune you out, and you never know which it will be. Some days, sitting right by her side and striking up a conversation, I have received back only a cold, dead stare. Those times, Alma manages to hold an expression so still, not even blinking her eyes, that I begin to believe she can't hear or see me. That is, until she snaps to and calls out a hello to another who may pass by or come to sit by her other side.

Alma's been diagnosed with "undifferentiated schizophrenia," though some in the know believe she is "mentally retarded," not schizophrenic. Sometimes it is difficult to tell the two conditions apart, especially when street drugs are added to the mixture.

The first time we have a semblance of a conversation, Alma insists on calling me "Chris." For months afterwards, I am Chris. I even learn to look up whenever I hear someone call, "Hi, Chris!" That day, we talk about the new shoes a friend has given her. They are a little too small for Alma's feet, but she likes them anyway. They are brand new, never worn by anyone else before, and have a strap across the front. Alma especially likes the strap and tells me so several times.

Most often, our chats are like that—brief and repetitive. Each time we speak, I ask if she'd like to come to the cooking group. Each time, Alma declines the invitation.

Things change after I start with the camera. Alma wants me to take her picture, and another one and another one. I have lots of pictures of Alma. Each time I bring in a new batch of prints, Alma is off, showing them to anyone in the house who will give her half a minute. I frame her favorite one and give it to her as a gift. Alma is thrilled. She kisses me a half dozen times and holds onto me for a long, lingering hug. I can feel how thin and frail she really is. All that day, Alma could be heard, "Chris, thank you for the picture, Chris. Thank you for the picture."

Dominique doesn't want me to take her photograph today. I'm surprised, since Dominique, with her dramatic eyes, dramatic laugh, dramatic saunter, has always been ready to ham it up for the camera.

"Dresden told me I'm *fat*," Dominique explains. "She said I'm so fat I'm an *embarrassment,* and *she'd* never take me anywhere with *her*. She said, 'How can you walk around with your huge belly and half the time it's not covered?'"

It's true that Dominique is a big woman. She is nearly six feet tall and weighs several hundred pounds. She seems comfortable with her size and stature. Will Dresden's insult change all that? Always statuesque, will Dominique now become ungainly?

The feud between the two women continues all day, until Dominique finally confronts Dresden. It turns out Dominique is getting pretty chummy with this guy named Gerald. Everyone knows each other from Fountain House, one of the places in the city people go to for "day programs." Patsy used to go out with Gerald before she became involved with Joseph, her fiance. After Patsy, Gerald began dating Dresden, but apparently they broke up. Rumor has it that Dresden still likes Gerald, and now she is very jealous that he has turned his attention to Dominique.

Dominique doesn't give a hoot why Dresden is picking on her. "I'm pissed at you," Dominique bellows at Dresden, "Just keep out of my face."

The boyfriend thing is a touchy issue. Although Dresden never married, her parents always intended she "marry and marry well and become a woman of advanced social standing." In fact, Dresden says, her mother was very specific in not teaching her daughter how to clean house. "She did not want me to do housekeeping chores," Dresden says. "My mother taught me how to tell other people to perform them for me." Dresden disappointed her parents on several counts. She never married, never had kids, never became a woman of advanced social standing, and she does her own housekeeping. Nevertheless, Dresden can't seem to resist keeping one eye on the lookout for Mr. Wonderful.

Dresden is classy and hip. Her family of origin hails from Jamaica and Barbados, although they've been settled in these parts all her life. Dresden describes her folks as "middle-class working people who valued frugality and were looking for economic and social security in the United States." That was no easy task. However noble may have

been the project of the parents, it was not without some unhappy consequences for the daughter. Their dreams remain
unfulfilled in her.

"I'm true to myself in the way I live my life," Dresden
says, to explain her youthful appearance. A vegetarian, she
eats properly and exercises, unlike virtually all the other
Woodhouse residents. A dancer and actress by training and
occupation, Dresden is one New Yorker who keeps up with
the arts. Drawn to the avant-garde, she seems to favor works
with political themes, for example, her favorite movies from
this year's film festival. There was the one about workers
in the South who had been literally locked into a chicken
factory by management seeking to prevent worker theft. A
fire broke out in the factory and the mostly women workers
perished at the locked door, found later to be scratched by
human fingernails as the workers tried clawing their way
out. And the one about the growing militancy of black identity and politics in Britain. And the one about distance and
relationship between a black woman in England and her
mother back home in the Caribbean.

Dresden's parents divorced when their only child was
still quite young. Before long, her mother remarried, this
time to "an American black from Virginia." A military man,
Dresden's stepfather moved his new family out of Brooklyn's
Bedford-Stuyvesant to Kansas. That's where Dresden had
her first real taste of American racism. A Catholic school
girl all her life, Dresden was unable to attend a Catholic school in Kansas since "it was all white and not yet
integrated."

Hers was a strict, repressed upbringing, and Dresden
wasn't always able to live "true to herself." She looks back
on an important turning point. At the time an enthusiastic
high schooler, Dresden announced her decision to become
a dancer. "'Only prostitutes become dancers,'" Dresden
recalls her stepfather commenting. The shamed teenager

was soon dismissed from the household, sent to boarding school for proper training.

All the years since, Dresden has carried the pain of this injustice and a plan to redress it. On her mother's deathbed, Dresden will ask her, "Why couldn't you have trusted me?" Dresden doesn't expect miracles from the confrontation. "They just think I'm not grateful," Dresden says of her parents' view of their daughter.

Dresden's depression comes and goes. Even so, Dresden managed to find her way to study dance and theater, and she has performed on stage and TV and in the movies. Most recently, Dresden performed in an off-Broadway play.

Like Dresden, Diane is a black woman in her fifties, but the two are as different as night and day. Diane is a soft-spoken mother of three who delights in her little grandson. A woman of simple tastes, Diane has a specific schedule to her day, which includes chores for Woodhouse's work program, her meals, and her favorite shows on the tube. She gets up very early in the morning, usually at five o'clock. By the time her soap operas come on, Diane is pretty much exhausted. Most afternoons, she has the TV tuned to channel seven: *All My Children, One Life to Live, General Hospital, Loving,* then *Oprah.* In the evenings after dinner, Diane follows a regular routine. First she takes her medications, then a shower. In the quiet of her room, Diane enjoys listening to her radio or watching TV, especially *Full House, Roseanne, Current Affair,* and "something about the FBI." Each night, Diane falls asleep to the sound of her radio. She describes the end of a typical day: "I listen to the news and also to know what time it is since I don't have a clock." On special occasions, she and Dixie go out for dinner at BBQs, Bill's, or Tad's Steak House on Thirty-fourth Street.

Diane has roots in the South, but she is unsure about
her family's background. "A woman" raised Diane and her
siblings, "not my real mother." Diane doesn't know if "the
woman" is a relative or not. All she knows is she was "very
abusive" and moved the young children from North Carolina to East New York in Brooklyn. Diane grew up believing
"the woman" was her mother but found out differently after
her twenty-seventh birthday, although she also says, "But I
knew it all along." Having been so deceived, Diane is no
longer sure what is or is not "true." She's not even sure she
was born in North Carolina.

"I was raised in a foster home." Of her "foster mother,"
Diane says, "she was a strict and moody woman" who
wouldn't allow young Diane to have any friends, but who
also raised two of Diane's three brothers and her sister.
The siblings are all now in their fifties, but there's trouble
amongst them.

Diane herself has three children. Her oldest is Dominick,
who lives in Virginia and works in the military. Willa is one
of Diane's two daughters. A single mother in her twenties,
Willa has a good job as a receptionist and an apartment of
her own she shares with her four-year-old son. Maybe twice
a year, Diane gets to visit them for the weekend. Diane
rarely sees her middle child, Marlys, who lives in Washington, D.C., and seems to be following in her mother's foot-
steps: Marlys has "been homeless, living in shelters."

Of her three babies, Diane raised only the boy. He was
born when Diane was just sixteen years old. Diane says the
others were taken in by "my people, by the older genera-
tion–cousins, uncles and aunts."

Diane is no longer interested in men and hasn't been with
one in fourteen years. That's when she stopped taking the
birth control pills she began using after her youngest was
born. Diane explains her indifference toward men. "I'm not

hot natured," Diane says, and besides, "all the men around here are trashy, like in shelters."

It's not that guys aren't interested in *her*. Not too long ago, Dominique broke off with fiance Anthony when he announced he liked someone else at Woodhouse. That someone was Diane. Next time he visited Woodhouse, Anthony called on Diane. "No way," Diane told Anthony, when he asked her out on a date.

Lynda Valentine is another Woodhouse woman who could care less about having a man in her life. "I doubt I would find anybody to go out with, have sex with," Lynda says. She has a lot more pressing issues on her mind. Like Diane, Lynda has had three babies, but "one son was murdered." Of his death, Lynda says, "All we know is he was shot by someone Spanish. He was twenty-one years old and no drugs, no gambling."

The past two years have been particularly rough for Lynda. Her son died, her mother died, three aunts died, her stepgrandmother died, and her uncle died.

Lynda missed the two most important funerals: her son's and her mother's. Lynda explains how this could happen: "I was moving from shelter to shelter at the time, nobody in the family knew how to contact me."

THE PLACE is abuzz with preparations for an upcoming protest trip to Albany. The new governor has some slashing in mind, and the Woodhouse budget is one of its likely victims. Lately, the news gets worse and worse. Only a few weeks ago, the issue made page one of the New York Times.

Pataki in Switch, Seeks Cuts in Programs for the Mentally Ill

Albany. Fifteen months ago, Senate Republicans, including George E. Pataki, spearheaded the passage of landmark legislation that was intended to revolutionize care for the mentally ill and reduce the number of sick, disoriented people living on the streets.

The new law requires the state to begin closing its expensive and largely anachronistic psychiatric hospitals and to use the savings to expand a broad range of community mental health programs. For three decades, the state had been emptying its psychiatric hospitals, then using the savings to help balance its budget, leaving thousands of former patients homeless and without treatment.

Now, just as the first dollars have started to flow to day treatment programs in Brooklyn and group homes in Buffalo, Governor Pataki has proposed repealing vital parts of the law and making large cuts in the very community programs that he and his fellow Republican senators had pressed Gov. Mario M. Cuomo to enact.

At the same time, he would continue to shrink the number of state hospital beds by ten percent, a move that advocates for the mentally ill say is a prescription for more homelessness. (Sack 1995)

A sign-up sheet for the bus to Albany is tacked on the bulletin board. Tomorrow, the full bus will carry one contingent among a larger group advocating the preservation of mental health services.

A group of us sit around the smoking table, just outside the dining room. A platter serves as an ashtray, and it's filled to the brim with stale butts. I find it difficult to catch even a bit of fresh air in the smoking room, a narrow, windowless alcove. Under a new city smoking ordinance, the smoking room is not long for this world either.

Some of the volunteers for the Albany trip have politics in mind; others are going for the ride or to get away from the city. Diane decides not to go this time. In her view, she has taken such trips in the past to no avail. "I never saw the politicians I thought were going to be there," she explains. "We went to Albany when Cuomo was there, and we went to the capitol but he never came out. I never saw him and he never saw me."

Sol would very much like to take the trip, but personal concerns will stop her. Thinking about the long ride brings a worried look across her face. "Is there a toilet on the bus?" she wants to know. Her incontinence has only been getting worse, and Sol knows she can't stray too far from a bathroom.

Sol believes it is important the politicians understand the problems homeless people face. "There should be a school for homeless people," Sol says. "It would be like a village or a private school on a campus where they would have housing and food and classes. The young kids can learn what they need to learn not to be homeless in the future."

Explaining homelessness to politicians or even the general public doesn't always seem worth the effort. At least that's what some women think. Dixie has had many a moment of other people looking at her funny or throwing a rude remark her way, reactions that leave Dixie "feeling apart." An ordinary woman, Dixie says people think what they hear on the news–that she and others like her (homeless, mentally ill) are just "murderers." "There's a stigma," she says.

Dixie has a perfect recent example. Last November, she and a group of fellow residents had gone to vote at their local polling place, accompanied by Bill, a Woodhouse volunteer who helps out with special activities. As the women voted or waited their turn to vote, a polling place worker begins to eye Bill. She wants to know what he is up to, thinking maybe he is a loiterer. To Dixie's dismay, Bill all too carelessly answers, "I'm escorting these mentally ill women who are here to vote."

The incident doesn't end there. It gets worse. The polling place worker decides "these" women may not be competent to vote; after all, they are "mentally ill." According to Dixie, the worker "made the ladies sign an affidavit which says they'll agree that their vote may not count." Having already cast her vote, Dixie says she refused to sign the affidavit.

On their way back to Woodhouse, Dixie and the others gave the young volunteer hell. Dixie says Bill was filled with remorse, apologizing the whole way home.

"If I ever write my memoirs," Dixie sighs, "I'll call it *Pistachio Nuts*. When you eat them, they always leave a residue on your fingers, on your hands. Everything I've lived through has left a mark on me, just like pistachio nuts."

9

A Madness in Me

N ORA AND I sit in the dayroom, the TV tuned to a Joan Crawford melodrama. Miss Crawford is decked out in an incredible chiffon party dress and baubles. Nora and I think it's funny. Crystal says, "I wouldn't mind having a dress like *that*."

Now it's time for everybody's favorite soap opera. I remark on the sleazy appearance of the male character featured in today's episode. This comment prompts a discussion among several of us in the room. The fellow is sleazy—he's a rapist, and everyone knows it, including the young woman seducing him in the scene we are watching.

Finally, Susan and Clare, a case manager, bring in the groceries for today's cooking group. No one feels in the mood to cook, so the two women have brought back ingredients for hero sandwiches—roast beef, turkey, ham, cheese. The women open the food packages on the table, grab the luncheon meats, stuff them into their hero rolls, and eat. Soon almost nothing is left—no rolls, for example, by the time Nora comes into the dining room. Lillian, an elderly woman who doesn't "participate" in the cooking group in terms of helping out, is quick to grab a whole roll and stuff it with about a pound of different meats – not seeming to notice whether anybody else might want some too.

Lillian pulls out a couple of dollar bills from her house-coat. Slapping the bills into Nora's hand, Lillian says, "Go get me some stockings."

"Not now," Nora answers patiently. "I want to eat too."

Lillian dismisses Nora with a wave of her hand and insists the younger woman run the errand.

Nora tries a different tack. "You go, Lillian, the walk will be good for you."

Lillian doesn't go for Nora's suggestion and somehow per-suades Nora to run her errand.

Back at the table, Crystal wants to talk about "women's issues," but she can't think of a topic. Instead, we turn to the new resident of Woodhouse, a young Haitian woman named Annie Lafontant. Both she and Crystal wear their hair in cornbraids. After I compliment Crystal on her hairdo, I turn to Annie and say she looks beautiful. Annie breaks into a shy giggle and says, "When you say that, I feel like you're tickling me."

Somehow, the chitchat is now about rape. Considering how many of the women have experienced rape, I am not surprised the mood turns hostile when a group of women gather around a table and the talk turns to men. Susan tells us that she has sex with her imaginary husband, Tommy, but she sometimes cheats on him with her teddy bear. Su-san knows Tommy is imaginary, and that's just the way she wants to keep him. This way he's easier to manage, and Susan can always send him away when the mood strikes her. Fortyish Susan reveals that her only "sexual" experience oc-curred when she was eleven years old. That's when she was raped twice, by two different men. Since then, Susan makes love with only one "man"– Tommy.

Susan and Nora decide that if a man "rapes a child or a woman, he should be castrated." Susan wants to be sure we know what that means. "The man's penis should be cut off and don't forget about those testicles!"

Nora thoroughly agrees. "Cut the whole thing off!" she exclaims.

I ask, "Is this punishment for convicted rapists or anybody accused of rape?"

"Anybody accused of rape!" shouts a chorus of female voices.

"What if it was a mistake," I ask, "and the guy is innocent?"

Nora has a solution. "When they cut off their dicks, they can store them in jars and then if one got cut off by mistake, they can get the jar with the guy's dick and sew it back on!"

The hostility is catching and now we're all laughing. Susan's got a good one: "They can go to the cemetery and dig up an old dead man and use one of those!"

Reserved Hattie decides to join the party. "How about," she suggests, "all men have their penises cut off, whether or not they've raped?"

Annie joins us too. She just laughs. She tells us that she was almost raped once but she managed to escape from the guy in the nick of time.

Annie looks depressed, unhappy. I reach my arms out to hug her, and she lays her head on my shoulder while I stroke her back. Annie offers her sweet smile. I ask, "How are you doing? What's up? You seem upset."

As soon as I acknowledge her mood, she nearly bursts

into tears. "Things are really messed up," says the twenty-four-year-old college student. "I just want to get out of here."

Annie and I go out for a cup of coffee. Actually, Annie wants herbal tea because coffee makes her extremely depressed. She orders her tea and a carrot cake, which she doesn't touch. She arranges for the waiter to wrap it up. Maybe she'll be hungry later. She fills me in on some details of her life and on some of her concerns and worries about living at Woodhouse.

It wasn't until Annie Lafontant arrived at adolescence that things began to make sense, even though her life was a mess. Annie's family life wasn't exactly idyllic. She had grown up with a mother who kept her distance from Annie, treating the child "coolly." Annie says, "I was never cuddled by my 'mother.'" Her father didn't seem to want her around much either. Annie says he was very abusive, and beatings were not an irregular occurrence.

Annie describes her teenage years as "troubled." She was eleven the first time she ran away from home. "I don't remember where I'd go exactly"–Annie struggles to remember back only a decade or so–"but they'd always find me and send me back."

Arguments, fights, battles between father and daughter were common. During one particularly tough quarrel, the "truth" tumbled out. The woman Annie had for years called "Mommy" was not. Worse, "Mommy" was married to Annie's father when he stepped out for an extramarital romance. Then Annie came along, the "product" of this illicit affair.

Annie was fifteen when she heard the news, and two years old when her "real" mother died. Annie's been able to scrape together only bits of information here and there about her mother, learning some things from the woman's death certificate and more from long lost relatives. One thing is for certain. Annie's mother had come from Haiti to live and work as a maid in the United States. What were her dreams, Annie can only guess.

Annie continues her life history. "When my mother died, I was sent to Haiti, then back to the States." After shuttling between the two countries, the little girl finally settled in with her father and his wife in Brooklyn.

"It was a tough neighborhood," Annie recalls. "I learned people resolve their disagreements by physical force." At first, Annie found it difficult to get the hang of it, but she caught on by the time she entered junior high. She learned to show bravado and fight her way to acceptance. "No wonder," Annie notes, "I go into physical, screaming tirades when I'm angry."

The little girl grew into a troubled teen. A "runaway," the last time Annie left her folks was just before her "sweet sixteen." Soon afterward Annie found herself in a group home for youth. For Annie, the group homes "weren't bad," and she has fond memories of one place in upstate New York that gave Annie her own "little cottage in the country." It was pleasant and peaceful there, save for the fact that the young woman's father "never saw me or tried to get in touch with me" during those significant years.

Except once, when he called "because the group home wanted him to pay for me," Annie explains. At first she believed her father wanted to see her. "I was happy," she remembers feeling—until she discovered she was deluding herself. Annie now believes he sought her out and took her back into his home only because "he didn't want to pay for my special services." Anyway, this is what he told her. Once again, Annie was alone.

Annie has been struggling to make something of herself

in between tragedy and loneliness. At nineteen, she enrolled in a state university, hoping to study education and become a school teacher. That same year, her father died. Annie broke down. She became depressed. She became suicidal. She had a "breakdown." She failed her classes.

Not giving up hope entirely, Annie decided to head for Haiti in search of her lost family on her mother's side. She found three half-sisters, her mother's children. At first, her sisters were warm and welcoming. They bought her presents–expensive perfume and other trinkets–and Annie thought, "I found the nurturing family I always wanted." Before long, things soured there too. Her sisters' true motives for being nice became clear. Annie believes, "They were only being nice to me because they thought I could get them into the United States."

Haiti was the last straw, and Annie became "homeless." She was just twenty-one years old. For most of the next three years, Annie lived on the street and in subways, "but nobody around me knew I was homeless because of the way I look and keep myself." It is easy to see how this is true, observing her fresh-faced look, her just-right lipstick, and the trim skirt and sweater set she always wears.

During those three years, Annie frequented many a restaurant bathroom to keep clean and wash up. For the most part, she remained invisible and kept out of trouble. She was arrested only once. "You know," she begins the story, "those restaurants where you pay *after* you eat? Well, I went in and ordered lobster, but I didn't have any money to pay for it." Annie's little splurge cost her two weeks in a Long Island jail.

Annie also tried staying in a couple of municipal shelters. She considers shelters "horrible and dangerous" and found the streets "a safer bet." Over several months last winter, Annie lived in the subway.

"Oh, my God," I blurt out. "I can't believe you lived in the subway in the wintertime."

"It wasn't so bad," she answers. "The Number 7 train *is* pretty warm!"

Annie is tremendously concerned about living at Woodhouse. At times, she is overcome with a sense of dread and suffers a fear of being misunderstood and misinterpreted. "It's dangerous for me to live here because they can send you to a hospital or maybe prison," she says.[1] She doesn't know exactly what she should do. One side of her says to drop everything and move to Haiti, something she dreams of doing. The other side of her says to stay where she is, let Woodhouse help her get through her current financial difficulties, and stick with her plan to finish school. Annie is already enrolled in a college program. She still hopes to complete her degree in a few years and become a schoolteacher. Annie resigns herself to reality. "I guess I'll stay here for now. I'm borrowing money from Woodhouse and waiting for my public assistance to come through." Annie is firm in her decision not to apply for SSI because "I don't want my name to be in the computer, and I don't want to have problems in the future."

Annie has plenty of examples of just how risky living at Woodhouse can be. Recently, she met a young man who seemed interested in getting to know her better. When he called her at home, he got through to the main switchboard at Woodhouse. As he later reported to Annie, the young man made some inquiries about the residence and was told by the receptionist that "Woodhouse is a home for the mentally ill." Annie is devastated and deeply ashamed. "It should be up to me when and what I tell him about Woodhouse," she asserts, "and it's not that I was going to lie to him about my circumstances."

"I want to get out of here," Annie moans. "I can't stand

institutional living." She reports more incidents. The other day, she had an argument with Teri. Annie says Teri yelled at her for no good reason. Annie argued back. It escalated, and Annie began screaming and cursing at Teri. "I used the 'f' curse," Annie confesses. "And then I got in trouble. The staff told me I can't use language like that and get into fights like that." In her own home, Annie explains, "I wouldn't have to answer to anybody. It's not that I like walking around cursing at people or yelling at people, but in my own home, I'd be able to, without there being 'consequences.'"

Annie sets herself apart from the other women at Woodhouse. She insists, "I'm not like them, and I'm not mentally ill." Annie says they've put her on Haldol, an antipsychotic medication. She tries to hold back the tears. "I don't like the medicine," Annie cries. "I don't like its side effects and I don't always take it, even though they think I am." When she started taking the medicine, Annie didn't get her period for two months. That tells *her* something's not right with it.

Annie's chart reads like a textbook case of schizophrenia, mostly having to do with delusions, hallucinations, incoherence, and inappropriate affect.

Annie believes her behavior is odd only to North Americans. She insists that "a Haitian psychiatrist, knowledgeable in 'psychologie de Loa' would understand that I'm not insane or crazy." Episodes interpreted and treated as psychosis by those around her are to Annie simply a reflection of "a spiritual problem I need to work through." Annie says that during these so-called psychotic episodes, she is perfectly aware of what she is doing and what is happening all through it. "When I speak to myself in Creole," Annie tells me, "I'm just getting into my spiritual self. Any Haitian psychiatrist would be able to confirm that."

"I hate the food at Woodhouse," Annie once comments. "It's *foreign* food to me."

"MENTAL ILLNESS is part of the potential of the human condition," Sander Gilman observes. "It has many possible manifestations, many causes, many outcomes" (1988:16–17). That the women are captives of the mental health system as well as carriers of the stigma associated with mental illness are clearly two aspects of its many possible "outcomes."

Dixie tells us that people "think we're murderers."[2] If not imagined to be "mad-dog criminals," the mentally ill are, at the least, considered incompetent. Dixie's account of the group trip to the polls on Election Day attests to this point. "We are all afraid of these 'mad people,' as they have been called over and over in both the media and official pronouncements . . . and we must defend ourselves . . . against [them]," is Gilman's summary of the prevailing attitude (1988:16–17).

"Oh," Hattie sighs, "I'd like a man who is normal, not like me"; and Gilman notes, "No matter if we say that they live in their own world, the mentally ill do respond to this stereotyping of themselves." "I'm an odd woman," Felice tells us; and Gilman writes, "Since they must live in our world, the stereotype of madness dominates and shapes their realities" (1988:16–17). No wonder Annie is devastated, deeply ashamed when a gentleman caller is told that "Woodhouse is a home for the mentally ill."

Given the heavy load of ideology attached to schizophrenia, Annie cannot accept this diagnosis of her condition. She insists she is not like the rest of "them" and borrows from notions of cultural relativism to argue her case. To Annie, this mental illness is nothing more than a social construction. Annie denies its reality for herself, and she must therefore also reject Woodhouse, the means through which this "illness" would be constructed and become real. Annie does what Gilman warns us against: "The palpable signs of illness, the pain and suffering of the patient, cannot be simply dismissed as a social construction" (1988:9–10).

There is more. Annie is not afraid only of stigma, but dreads other consequences that would follow diagnosis. She refuses to be entered "into the computer [because] I don't want to have problems in the future." Annie does not want to surrender the little freedom and autonomy she retains. To accept Woodhouse's offer of help would be to step into the system and lose all control. As she puts it, "It's dangerous for me to live here, because they can send you to a hospital or maybe prison." After all, while the illness and its pain are real, how these are understood and handled is socially determined. Annie has perfectly valid concerns about the consequences of her diagnosis, though these might easily be dismissed as her "paranoia." Among the everyday results for the mentally ill, according to Gilman, is their "isolation as if they had contagion . . . and the sense that they form another world that is beyond, or below, or outside of our own" (1988:9–10).

If we can bear to hold onto this, Annie is at once mentally ill (schizophrenic, and she could benefit from the medication) and absolutely right to fear the institution and what its representatives can do to ruin the rest of her life. In the end, the pain of her illness cannot be denied (whether she admits it or not), and the system eventually takes her anyway. This is the tragic story of one young woman trapped by contradictions in the practice and ideology of mental illness.

10

Rage

Nora wants to take me out to lunch so I can have a taste of "soul food." We'll also stop by Visioncare on 125th Street to order her new prescription glasses.

On the way to and in the subway, Nora points to acquaintances she "runs with" when she's "on the street." There's the young woman sitting against a wall in the subway station, looking very pregnant and begging. "That's a fake belly," Nora divulges. We buy tokens, and Nora insists on paying. "I invited you," she reminds me. By the platform downstairs are four guys sleeping soundly on the benches. Nora knows them. "Most probably up all night hustling," she says, explaining why they are so exhausted. One fellow sells newspapers he steals off trucks, another picks up cans. They work very, very hard for the little they net in return. Nora says, "I don't have the patience to do the things they do for the money they get."

As usual, 125th Street is bustling. Visioncare is so crowded, it seems everyone on the avenue happens to need glasses today. Nora's a little edgy. She sees the long waiting lines and doesn't know if she wants to wait.

"What's the difference?" I ask her, "What else do we have to do? Where else are we going anyway?"

Nora concedes the point. She signs in and hands the clerk her lens prescription and small blue identification card.

"Let me see your Medicaid card," I say.

"Here." She offers it to me. "You white people've got the Gold Card, we got the Blue Card," Nora laughs.

The wait isn't long after all. Nora and I share a chair at the counter to choose just the right frames. The cabinet in front of us houses all the Medicaid frames. Nora takes a quick glance at the homely frames and bellows, "*I* don't like *these* frames, what *else* you have?"

The clerk doesn't seem to care whether or not Nora likes the frames or how loudly she says so. She indifferently takes us to another counter and makes sure Nora understands—she will have to pay for these.

Nora mutters to me, "If I'm not comfortable in 'em, I'll never use 'em."

We see all sorts of frames—red frames, blue frames, wire frames, tortoiseshell frames. Nora is confident in her likes and dislikes. Loudly she proclaims, "I don't *like* these. I don't like *these*, I don't like *these*."

The clerk brings out more and more styles. Finally we hear, "I *like* these," after but a glance in the mirror.

Nora had already gone to Sterling Optical near Woodhouse, where she found a great pair of glasses priced at $139. She was hoping to do better here. The clerk offers Nora "cheaper" frames, starting at $89. The ones she wants cost $114. Nora thinks Jeanne wouldn't approve of her spending so much money; the case manager buys her own frames for $30 downtown on Orchard Street.

"I'll take them," Nora tells the clerk as she hands over a $50 down payment.

Back on 125th, Nora wants to find a certain restaurant. It's around here someplace, but Nora can't remember the name or where it is exactly. I suggest we ask someone. Nora turns to the first person who passes. "Excuse me, you know a soul food restaurant around here?"

The dark-skinned Spanish woman seems to have no idea what Nora is talking about. She shrugs and goes on her way.

Next we spot a police officer patrolling the corner. Nora does the talking. "Excuse me, officer," she says politely, "do you know of a soul food restaurant around here? I know it used to be here."

Yes, he tells us, there's a place just around the corner. Thank you very much, and we turn to leave. "Excuse me," the officer says to me. "Are you here with her?" As if I don't belong.

"Yes," I answer politely. "I'm here for a visit."

"Oh,"–the cop smiles, trying to look his handsome best– "I'm pleased to meet you." He extends his hand toward mine. As our hands clasp, the officer turns to Nora. "Now you bring your friend back here when you're done with your lunch." He winks.

Nora and I back away. We know to say "ha-ha-ha" and wave cheerfully.

She can't wait to rub it in. So everyone can hear, she hoots, "He's trying to pick you up! He likes you! Officer Barrett likes you!"

"How do you know his name?" I come back at her.

"First thing I do is look at their name," she says. It's a matter of common sense.

The restaurant is self-serve, except for the chitterlings, which the cook behind the counter serves you from a big, black pot. These days, Nora hears, it can cost $15 for a plate of chitterlings in Harlem. This place isn't that expensive.

Nora orders the chitterlings with collard greens, macaroni and cheese, and a ginger ale. I take some chicken, sweet potatoes, fried plantains, and a Diet Coke. Nora watches over me like a mother hen—I take too little of this, too much of that. Now I eat too fast, now too slow.

I taste her chitterlings and collard greens before she smothers them in salt, her habit with most food. I think it's got too much oil, but she disagrees. She can't wait to dig in. "I've been dying for this food," she tells me, recalling the days when her father did the cooking for the family.

Speaking of food, Nora says, "Did I tell you I'm gonna be feeding 'the homeless'? I'm gonna work for the 'homeless' 'cause I was once 'homeless' too." (Amazingly, Nora is able to simultaneously capture a do-gooder's persona while mocking the paternalism inherent in such helping deeds.)

Something inspired her to go to the church near Woodhouse and talk to the priest about volunteering on Saturday mornings. "I see them all lined up for food," she tells me. "My friends."

"Great," I say, encouraging her.

"Yeah, yeah," she says. "They'll see me there and probably ask me to hang out with them, and I'll try hard not to go."

THE NEXT TIME I come to Woodhouse, Gus tells me he hasn't seen Nora for days. "She's decompensating," he concludes with maybe a little too much certainty. I feel my face flush. Has Nora hit the streets again?

At least cooking was canceled for the day. The stove isn't working, and we have to wait until the kitchen is scrubbed up. It seems Annie was given special permission to use the library to study, now that she's in school. Turns out, Annie didn't study at all. Instead, she used the kitchen to "cook herself a three-course meal." Apparently, Annie splattered grease all over the stove, including the pilot light. Gas was escaping, and the pilot light had to be turned off.

Annie cooked herself rice and beans, and she left behind a mess of pots and pans. In fact, the kitchen looks pretty filthy, worse than ever. Annie's privileges were revoked.

I hear that Annie fell apart the other day, almost completely. Her case manager discovered Annie had been "cheeking her meds for two months." On Tuesday, Annie became hysterical. Once again, she manifested what those around her consider to be bizarre behavior–shaking uncontrollably while hurling foul-mouthed insults at anyone in her path. That day, Annie was given the choice to either take her medication or be hospitalized.

They say she's a paranoid schizophrenic. I hear that's the "best" kind of schizophrenia to have–the one with "the best outcome" and the one that "goes into remission more often than the other forms." I manage to get hold of the pay-phone number on Annie's floor in the "psyche ward" at Bellevue. The message is always the same. "Annie doesn't want to come to the phone," they tell me.

I can't get Nora off my mind, and Gus agrees to ring up her room. She's there! I can come up if I want to. The five flights to her floor seem endless. I know Nora always runs up and down these steps without skipping a beat or a breath. But by the third floor, I need to take a rest.

Nora hears me as soon as I step on the landing. She calls for me and I walk toward the room with the door ajar.

She looks so skinny, sickly. She's lying in bed and apologizes for the mess in her room. "You look so skinny," I say as I stroke her face, rub her back.

"I feel so bad, so bad." She had screamed at Jeanne and then broken the fan in the corner of Jeanne's office. Now Jeanne wants her to see the psychiatrist tomorrow, and she doesn't want to. She doesn't want to do anything anymore or see anyone anymore. Nora thinks about what she did to Jeanne.

"I don't want anybody to see me like that. You don't know what I'm really like. You haven't seen this side of me.

"I'm so filled with *rage*. When it comes over me, I can't control it."

NORA'S RAGE. Is it possible that all of Nora's therapists are so intent on "fixing" her they cannot "see anger as a blessing instead of as an illness," as Emily Martin suggests? To see it as a blessing, Martin argues that "it may be necessary for women to feel that their rage is legitimate. To feel that their rage is legitimate, it may be necessary for women to understand their structural position in society, and this in turn may entail consciousness of themselves as members of a group that is denied full membership in society simply on the basis of gender. If [social] causes are at the root of the unnamed anger that seems to afflict women, and if they could be named and known, maybe a cleaner, more productive anger would arise from within women, tying them together as a common oppressed group instead of sending them individually to the doctor as patients to be fixed" (1987:135).

The way I see it, misogyny is only one of many factors that contribute to the "abuses of the spirit" with which all the Noras contend. It's the totality of their various experiences with homelessness, mental illness, racism, and poverty that make for what Kleinman calls "the 'soft knife' of routine processes of ordinary oppression" (1996:xi).

Along with everything else, then, Nora struggles with her addiction. After the last "relapse," Nora's been "into" her "sobriety" only about five weeks now. After each relapse, the counting starts again. Sometimes it's eighty-one days, sometimes fifty-seven. In between, Nora goes to AA, NA, her psychiatrist, her counselor, and her case manager.

This one happened a couple of weeks ago. She was in bed. It was night and Nora hates the night time. She couldn't sleep, tossing and turning. The little white rocks just waiting for her down the street.

She gets up and out the door again. "Finally I said, 'Fuck it,' and about two o'clock in the morning I was up and dressed and out of there, and before you know it, I was drinkin' and druggin' again. I hate myself for this. I feel so bad."

It's just she gets so lonely and somehow gets it into her head that drink and drugs will fill up that loneliness. The key is somewhere in these deepest feelings.

Nora stayed a couple of nights in the park. Central Park, Riverside Park. She prefers Riverside. Just this past day or two, they found a couple of women killed in Central Park. "That doesn't scare me enough to stop what I'm doing," she tells me, shaken by her own recklessness. Nora is ashamed. "Victoria saw me on the street with a bottle of Chablis in a paper bag." She stops talking and looks away from me. "It wasn't really Chablis, it was Thunderbird. I said Chablis so you don't think I'm nothing but a drug addict and a drunk."

Meanwhile, she keeps asking, "Now what are you going to think of me?" and "Are you going to leave me?" I must have been in her room for an hour. She hasn't had any alcohol or cocaine in two days. They've given her a sedative to help her sleep. I remind her that her body is coming down from all these chemicals. Crashing feels lousy.

She wants to know if I am going to the cooking group and

seems disappointed when I tell her it's canceled for the day.
Maybe she does want to come out of her room after all, see
people.

We go to the bodega for some food. I wish she'd get
chicken soup, but Nora buys a coke, two bags of candy, and
potato chips. I go to the back of a long line to pay while Nora
waits at the front of the store. She calls for me when they
open a second register. I make my way to the head of the
new line when someone yells at us for cutting in. Nora
answers back, loud and menacing. I snap at her between
clenched teeth, "What do you care what that woman says,
thinks of you?" Nora laughs, squeezing my hand. She can't
help but engage every time.

As we leave, an older gentleman, well-dressed and well-
groomed, passes us. He gestures to Nora as we walk by. She
pulls my arm and whispers that he's looking for dope. "Last
week I was selling," she confides. Not only that, she was
nearly arrested. "Now what do you think of me?" she wants
to know.

It happened just across the street, on the corner where
she was "pitching bundles." The bundles go for about fifty
dollars and she gets about four dollars for each one she
sells. In one two-hour period, Nora managed to sell about
ten to twelve bundles and earned a good sixty-five dollars,
about a 12 percent cut.

"I was on the corner and these young, Spanish guys–they
were Dominicans or Colombians, I think–they were there
too. I got the bundles from them. All of a sudden, the cop car
was there and two officers came out. Everybody scattered
except me. I just stood there, a bundle in my hand. I slipped
it under a car, but I still had the money in my pockets. The
cops says, 'We'll let you go, if you answer two questions for
us.' I said, 'Yes, officer.' First question is, 'Where's the bundle?'
I showed him. The cop said, 'Very good. Now question num-

ber two, who're you selling for?' I says, 'Oh, officer, you know who I'm selling for–those young Spanish guys you seen on the corner with me.' So the officers let me go. I was lucky, but I'm not goin' out there again because my luck won't hold.

"So I walked uptown a bit to get a beer, and I see the Spanish guys. I told them I'm not gonna sell no more. I asked them, 'Why you just run away like that, leaving me with the cops?'"

"Did they get mad when you said you weren't going to sell for them anymore?" I ask.

"Naw," she says. "They'll just go get someone else to pitch for them."

Just then Jeanne walks by. She doesn't see us because we're in the corner store buying plums.

Nora looks down and whispers, "She hates me."

11

Difference and Other
Infections of the Day

SONIA MORALES is crouched against the wall just
outside Woodhouse. The skinny, sickly woman cradles her
arms, rocking back and forth, eyes barely open. I think, "She
will be dead soon." [1]

With all the people buzzing up and down the street, it is
easy to miss the small, insignificant figure.

It's been months since Sonia was evicted from Woodhouse. She's been seen in the neighborhood several times.
This day, she returns to a familiar spot, maybe to find some
small comfort.

Inside, Crystal prepares fried beef and broccoli with rice
and soy sauce, and a salad on the side. Though she compe-
tently goes through all the motions, Crystal's not really into
cooking today. "I'm so fat," she complains. A holiday is coming up, and Crystal was looking forward to wearing a beautiful black velvet dress she hasn't yet had a chance to wear.
This morning, she tried it on and her day was ruined. "It
doesn't fit at all," she tells us, "None of my party dresses fit."

Everyone else is still excited about the film crew that had
been at Woodhouse "to make a movie." It's been almost two

weeks since the film crew has come and gone, but the thrill remains. Well, it isn't exactly a movie, but a public service announcement arranged by Woodhouse fund-raisers. The PSA features Woodhouse and airs on TV for months. The crew had been to Woodhouse weeks ahead of time to talk to the women and scout out the site. Nora had been chosen to be the star of the thirty-second spot. Victoria worries and wonders if the pressure to perform triggered Nora's latest "relapse."

The shoot was scheduled, and no one knew if the star would show. But, even in the depths of her despair, Nora hadn't let them down. In fact, Nora, at once poignant and cool, sophisticated, intelligent, and street wise, gave a stellar performance. "I didn't want to disappoint Victoria," she tells me at the table.

The shoot was quite amazing. The crew, the cameras, the action, and all the excitement. They made such a big fuss and lavished enormous attention on Nora. "They talked to me, interviewed me for so long, longer than anyone else," Nora crows.

The makeup lady was everyone's favorite. By the time she was done, all of Woodhouse's actresses looked incredible. Makeup took very good care of each performer–Teri, Diane, Denise, Nora.

"It was *nice,*" smiles Diane.

The conversation reminds me of something Dixie told me about depression. She was hospitalized twice when "it got really bad." I wondered what happens in the hospital that is different from the outside. In depression, Dixie explains, "the first thing that goes is I don't bathe, I don't change my clothes, I don't do my hair." In the hospital, Dixie says, "I don't have to take care of myself. I'm taken care of until I can do it myself."

Imagine a full-time makeup lady at Woodhouse.

While we wait for Crystal to serve the meal, the young volunteer, Charisse, pulls out the latest issue of *Essence* magazine. She turns to a reader's sex survey and says we should do it. She asks me to read the questions aloud.

"Question one," I read. "What was your age of first sexual intercourse?"

"Does that mean kissing," asks the teen worker, "or what?"

"No, no," answer Crystal and Nora in unison, "it means *sex* sex."

"Oh," says Charisse, who adds that she hasn't had "*sex* sex yet."

Next question. "How often do you have sex?"

Crystal can't wait to answer, "Every day," she says, "I'd like to have sex every day."

Charisse looks confused. "It doesn't ask you how much you *want*, but what the *truth* is. How much do you have sex?" Crystal doesn't get it.

Finally, Nora asks, "Crystal, how often do you see Raymond?"

"Four times a week," she answers.

"Do you have sex with him each time you see him?" comes the followup.

"Yeah." Crystal giggles coyly.

"Why do you want to have sex every day?" Charisse wants to know.

"Because he has a long dick!" Nora answers, goofing on Crystal.

"Yeah," Crystal agrees, "it's like this long," as she puts up her hands to show us all how incredibly long she means. Crystal and Raymond don't bother with foreplay. "We go straight for intercourse," she says. "All that kissing and stuff isn't important anymore." Crystal's into talking. "My only complaint is he comes too fast, but I have an orgasm every time I have sex with Raymond and my body, it twitches for ten minutes!" Crystal shows us, squirming and shivering in her seat.

"How often does your partner perform oral sex on *you?*" is the next question.

"I don't mind oral sex," Crystal confides, "except when Raymond comes in my mouth. I don't like *that.*"

Crystal takes the next question too. "Do you tell your partner what you want in sex?"

"Well, Raymond wants me to do something I don't want to do," Crystal says. "Anal sex." Crystal giggles nervously. "I had an old boyfriend who did that to me once, and I hated it. It hurt so much, I cried out, 'Mercy Jesus!' I don't want to do it, but Raymond keeps asking."

"No way," says Nora. "Anytime a man used to come up to me and say he's gonna have sex in my behind, I tell him, 'Hell no, not me–you're not putting your penis in my behind.' I never heard of stuff like that. That scared the hell out of me because a penis don't belong in your backside. It's sick, it's crazy."

"Why do men like that nasty stuff?" Crystal wants to know.

"It's tight!" Charisse blurts out. By now, all us women are guffawing. Even the silent Sharlea breaks into a little smile.

"WHAT COMES to mind when you hear the words 'AIDS' or 'HIV'?" I've been asking around the house, even though

I am well aware that HIV risk and the barriers to reducing risk for women like those who come to live at Woodhouse has only partly to do with their attitudes and beliefs about the disease. Bigger, more complicated factors also position people to become "at risk" for AIDS: poverty, the lack of affordable and adequate housing, limited access to preventive health and mental health care, the consequences of institutionalized care, and, on an individual level, the deepest psychological aspects of feeling (Odets 1994, 1995; Waterston 1997).

Because my project at Woodhouse began as AIDS-related research, I worry about its focus on a "targeted group." AIDS researcher Stephanie Kane has chronicled her struggle with these issues. "I have been working in tense relation to a categorized risk group, at once working within and against categories in the representational struggle for resources," Kane writes of the dilemma (1993:225). Kane's dilemma resonates with my own. The tension comes from the likelihood that images already associated with "mentally ill," "homeless," "minority," "women" will infiltrate the new disease and our prevention efforts (Gilman 1988; Treichler 1988). After all, before the advent of AIDS, this "categorized risk group" had already been constituted.

Indeed, in the relatively short history of the AIDS epidemic, the process of "infiltration" is well underway (Gilman 1988; Treichler 1988; Glick Schiller 1992; Crawford 1994). Gilman notes that, in the early days of the epidemic, the origin of the disease was "located within the paradigm of American racist ideology" (1988:263; see also Farmer 1992). Similarly, Crawford observes that "the 'unhealthy,' 'contagious,' 'sexually deviant,' and 'addicted-minority' other [are] all condensed in the negative symbolism of AIDS." In the cultural politics of AIDS, the healthy (the "good," "respectable," "responsible") are differentiated from the diseased; in turn, these images are tied to dominant ideologies about race, class, and sexuality (1994:1347–1348).

Crawford also suggests ways in which these images have real, painful consequences for those on the other side of good (1994:1363). The elements of harm include fear, blame-the-victim ideologies, the denial of human suffering, and the enactment of punitive measures. At the very least, it is imperative that those designing AIDS-prevention programs be conscious of these social processes. For the women of Woodhouse, we must provide AIDS prevention without adding fuel to the fire of the underclass script, and without causing more suffering to come their way.

I turn to the women for answers. What I get is as varied as the women themselves. Sophia Barnes and I sit on the park bench that furnishes the outdoor patio at Woodhouse. When she hears the words AIDS and HIV, she says, "I think of America."

"What do you think about having a woman's group here to talk about AIDS and HIV?" I probe.

Not necessary, according to Sophia, since the disease is "not prevalent here." She explains further: "They don't have it here. HIV is impossible to get. It's only contractible with an American man."

"We're in Yugoslavia," Sophia reminds me. "It's impossible for us to get the disease."

In our conversation about HIV infection, Denise's thoughts drift toward her daughter, Renee. What with Renee's crack use, boyfriends, and four kids, Denise worries that her daughter is not taking the proper precautions to avoid getting the disease. The problem is, according to Denise, "you don't have the chill factor on AIDS"–there is no cure for this disease.

Denise, who has substance abuse problems herself, considers her own needs very different from those of Renee, in part because of their location in the life cycle. As Denise puts it, "Women are at different levels, at different stages of life, and it's so important. Some women want kids, some don't want kids, some are in menopause, some are not." For herself, Denise explained, "I can have as much sex as I want 'cause I'm in menopause."

In fact, Denise hasn't had sex in three years. If she were to have sex with someone now, "he'd have to show me he's not HIV positive, show me papers from his doctor, it's mandatory for me." On second thought, Denise says, "I may get caught though–I may get hot in a situation. I'd have the man use a condom, but I might just do it anyway. It's easy to say you would use a condom than actually use it. It's like saying I'll skip birth control for one day and wind up pregnant."

In the past, Denise used two forms of birth control–the pill and douching. "I didn't use a diaphragm 'cause I couldn't focus on that thing–it's clumsy and I couldn't see it. But I used to douche after sex every time–even when I was on the street I had to douche. I'd use plain soapy water and kept my douche right here," Denise says, pointing to the fanny pack she wears around her waist. "When I had a home, I used vinegar and water, the way my mother and grandmother taught me. Even when I was living with my man, he told me to do it–to douche. It was like clockwork."

Sharlea also douches regularly. She averages about once a month, but it is not related to her menstrual cycle or sex. Recently, she began using Massengill to douche because "I wanted to feel clean."

Likewise, Teri douches once a month, "but only once, af-

ter my period, because I don't want to upset my Ph balance."
When Teri thinks of "unsafe sex," she wonders about "female to female love."

When Nora hears the words "HIV" or "AIDS," she can't
help but worry about a lot of things she has done over the
years. Thinking back on her days on the street, Nora says, "If
I walked out the door and I ran into somebody who was
gonna get me high for free, then I didn't have to have no sex.
It wasn't a regular thing. It depends on the day. It depends on
the people you run into. And when you're homeless, you
can't go and douche all the time. A man could use a rubber
and he takes the rubber off and puts it in the garbage, you
know, like that. But a woman is the one that always has to
douche—you don't walk around with all that stuff in you, you
know. When you're homeless, you did the best you can.
When you got your period, if you didn't have anybody get
napkins, there was always tissues, there were always tissues. It was hard, it was hard. I'm telling you, it wasn't easy.
There were times when I had blood on my panties because
you would forget that today is period day. So you tried your
best to go to the bathroom, remove your clothing, and try
your best to pad yourself well with tissues, with toilet tissue.
Listen, when you're homeless, it ain't about trying to be
Miss Lady Vanderbuilt."

Nora talks about her new projects. She had recently been
chosen to be part of an AIDS study, another Columbia University project similar to the one that brings me to Woodhouse. "I was at the Ryan," she says excitedly. "They were
looking for people 'randomly,' is what they said." The year-
long project is all about sex, drugs, and AIDS.

"They asked me a lot of questions about sex and drugs,"
she says, when I ask her to describe what she's done so far.

"I always wondered if people answer those surveys truthfully or not," I tell her. "How did you answer the questions, truthfully or not so truthfully about every thing?"

"All of them truthfully," she affirms, "'cause they told me that the study will help other people, and I want to help other people so I told the truth." She'll be spending four hours a week for the next seven weeks on the project and then that much time again a little way down the road.

She loved the first group. She reenacts the session, portraying all four characters. The leader was a guy named Andy, a former addict who is HIV positive. "I can't use their real names," she tells me. "They said everything in the group is confidential."

"Andy had each of us say one thing positive we'd done since the new year and why we're here in the group. He went first. He said he was there to help other people learn about AIDS and HIV.

"Then Cindy went. She said, 'I've been married for eight years or twelve years to this man who's been cheating on me.' She caught him cheating on her with another woman. This Cindy, she was very upset 'cause she'd been having sex with her husband without a condom so maybe now he's given her AIDS. So she went and got tested and she's negative. She's relieved since she's got two kids. Cindy said the positive thing she'd done this year is 'get rid of my husband,' who is no longer in her life. Cindy told us if she had been positive, she would've written a will for someone to take her kids, give the will to her mother, and then kill herself.

"This other lady, Melinda, said she had just come out of jail where she had been locked up for a year on drug charges. She said the positive thing she did was come to this meeting.

"Then this other lady, Ann, said she has a boyfriend and they don't use condoms but she doesn't think she has to be worried about AIDS 'cause she believes her boyfriend would tell her if he was sleeping with, wanted to sleep with somebody.

"Cindy, with the cheating husband, told her, 'How can you trust any man? You can't trust any man and I know 'cause of my husband.' And Ann got mad, she was thinking Cindy insulted her boyfriend!"

According to Nora, the group covered all sorts of great topics. Myths and truths about HIV and AIDS. All different stuff about sex, and different kinds of condoms. Nora gives some more details. "I didn't realize a person with HIV can look healthy—they don't have to look sickly. I always thought they had to look sickly. Also, if a woman is positive and she's pregnant, it doesn't mean the baby is automatically gonna get HIV.

"They showed us all kinds of condoms, and they had penis models so we could practice putting condoms on it. They said that if you had a choice between a lambskin condom and nothing, which would you use? And the answer is to the lambskin condom. It's not the best condom, but it's better than nothing.

"There were ribbed condoms, which they said was good for vaginal sex. They said the ribbed part helps stimulate the woman. There were flavored condoms, good for oral sex."

"What flavors did they have?" I ask.

"Mint," she answers deadpan, and we laugh. "And *straw-berry*," she laughs, licking her lips.

"They told us," Nora continues, "they used to think that anal sex was the most dangerous and oral sex was not so dangerous. Now they're saying it's all dangerous. With oral sex, there's still secretions and maybe menstrual blood. You know, I don't believe that a penis goes in my backside, that's what I would tell them. But there are people who like it. There are women who like that, you know. And there are

women out here who don't use drugs, who don't use alcohol
who like all types of sex.

"I loved it at the group 'cause I got the chance to talk
about all my confused feelings about sex. It's a small group
and I can talk about these private things. They're teaching
me things I should've learned years ago from my parents,
like about masturbation. I had a lots of teachings as a Catholic schoolgirl and I have guilt and certain desires.

"I've never had sex without drugs. Sex comes in 'cause of
drugs. Sometimes—a lot of times—it's to get drugs. Sometimes it's for desire, but drugs are always there too. I wish I
could have sex for desire, without drugs in the picture. Another thing with drugs in the picture is you get sloppy."

"What do you mean, 'sloppy'?"

"Not responsible, not using protection."

In my conversation with Diane, she says, "I don't understand AIDS" and recalls the time she took a test for AIDS.
"I haven't had no boyfriend, no men in fourteen years, and I
don't use drugs. I'm gonna take another AIDS test, but in the
first test there was nothing wrong with me.

"I'd feel safer if I took the test again," she reasons.

For Sarah, "AIDS is something that is usually degenera-
tive in a two-year time period and a breakdown of the system where you lose your strength. I understand it is ram-
pant not only among the gay community but those who use
drugs and have promiscuous sex."

For Patsy, AIDS "is just a sad thing." She also thinks of
people dying, of people using needles. Patsy says that God
doesn't like women to be with women and men to be with
men. "The Lord made man and woman, not man and man,
or woman and woman," the Woodhouse spiritualist explains. According to Patsy, things like drugs and AIDS were
"all foretold in the Bible." Still, she admonishes, "It's important to remember people who passed on."

Lynda has someone to remember. After she and her husband split up, Lynda "lived with someone for ten years, and he died of AIDS. I didn't know he had AIDS."

Lynda has been tested for HIV, but not because of her long-term companion. "I took a test in order to stay in the shelters," she explains. The thing is, Lynda didn't know the fellow had AIDS when she was with him. "He got it from someone else," she found out later, long after they had already stopped seeing each other. In fact, Lynda only knew about his illness from friends. "They said he was dead," she recalls. "I had no idea he had AIDS," Lynda says. "You never know."

Hattie thinks of all the people going around without taking precautions. For herself, it's not an issue, because she "never took illegal drugs, never used needles or cocaine." Not that she's interested, but "if I start dating, if by any chance I'm all mellowed out because of my age, I would never have sex without precautions."

"What do you mean by 'precautions'?" I want to know.

She heard all about it on WBAI, the famous New York City "listener-supported" radio station. "About six months ago on 'BAI," she informs me, "they had the most interesting evening. Women—in addition to a man wearing a condom— a woman can be thoroughly sheathed with something that covers the vagina and outside of the vagina, so there's no disease like syphilis or gonorrhea or AIDS. It was such a comfort to know about that. I don't know what it was called, but if I needed it, I would ask a doctor for it—it's something new."

Dominique has her own strategy for avoiding HIV. First of all, for years, she's been lucky. "I never used protection and I've never gotten pregnant," Dominique is proud to say. She has never had any kind of venereal disease, only some minor yeast infections. In terms of AIDS prevention, Dominique's special method is to be "careful who I choose. I choose those I think are clean. I check 'em out and ask 'em if they had a disease."

Tanya, who recently announced her engagement to Murray, carries condoms in the fanny pouch she wears around her waist most times. She and Murray have been talking about having children someday. They are thinking maybe to adopt. The future is a little uncertain, what with their housing situation, and now Murray has "full-blown AIDS." "Before he met me," Tanya explains, "he'd gone out with men."

Murray hasn't been doing very well lately. Tanya says he is often tired and tires easily. He can't eat and he's already been in the hospital a couple of times. When Murray goes to the day program where the couple met, he is often unable to participate in any of the activities. Instead, he will lie across some chairs while the others hang out, talk, play cards.

ALL THIS VARIETY—of experiences, remarks, attitudes, and beliefs—shows that our social categories rest on shaky ground. Indeed, Woodhouse women challenge the whole tendency to classify—to make and live by social categories. "Complexity is erased by the very categories of difference we are given," notes Rayna Rapp, and the categories lead both to stereotyping and to programs based on false assumptions (1995:178). To illustrate, I have heard the following remarks in discussions among AIDS-intervention specialists: "Hispanic women won't touch their vaginas," and "Since black women refuse to insert objects into their vaginas, they will never use something like the female condom."

Instead of designing interventions by social category, wouldn't it be better to design AIDS-prevention programs informed by "embodied experience," tailored, say, to "the woman in the body" (Martin 1987; Cassell 1996)? Ideally, such a program would take into account the *whole* of women's experiences, including their biological, psychological, and social aspects (Stein 1990, 1993, 1995; Krieger and Zierler 1995; Schneider and Stoller 1995; Doyal 1995). This means the kind of comprehensive program that requires a financial, political, and ideological commitment, the kind that does not currently exist. Indeed, at this political-economic juncture, human needs, particularly for poor people, are barely on the agenda (Farmer, Connors, and Simmons 1996).

"What comes to mind when you hear the word 'AIDS' or 'HIV,'" I ask Debra Brown.

Debra shrugs her shoulders. "That I'll be dying soon," she answers with a quiet smile.

12

The Road to Clarity

IN THE LAST weeks before she leaves Woodhouse
for good, Alma starts coming to the cooking group. She always helps out, clearing and washing dishes. The day she
tells me about her kids is the day I play head chef. Roast
chicken is on the menu, and I delight in cooking up the livers
for Alma.

Today I get as much of her story as I ever will. The thirty-
nine-year-old woman was born and raised in the Bronx and
has a twin sister whose name is also Alma. She has three
daughters, ages five, eighteen, and twenty-one years. The
baby, her name is Alma too.

"How old were you when you had your babies?" I ask
Alma.

"I was twelve when my oldest daughter was born," she
tells me, "I was fifteen when I had the second one, and I was
seventeen when I had the third one."

That would mean her kids are now twenty-two, twenty-
four, and twenty-seven years old. Maybe the two older girls
were eighteen and twenty-one the last time she saw them.
Maybe the youngest was five the last time she saw her.

THE HOUSE is beginning to smell deliciously of garlic
and onions melting in sweet cream butter. Sophia Barnes,

189

a relatively recent arrival from a downtown city shelter, comes in briefly to check out what's cooking. A faded beauty, Sophia is a straggly blond who wears lots of lipstick and a short, tight skirt. She surveys the bookshelves and pulls out a trashy romance novel.

Sophia's looking great, actually. When she first arrived at Woodhouse a few months earlier, the quiet woman appeared bewildered, disoriented. It didn't help her appearance that dark roots had grown into the blond hair plastered flat against the top of her head, brown and yellow bangs covering her eyes. Today I barely recognize her. With a new wash, cut, and dye, Sophia looks like a different person. Her hair is pulled away from her face, and for the first time, I see that Sophia has lovely blue-green eyes.

Sophia's not particularly interested in any of the food I prepare, although the livers sautéing in butter and onions lure even those most resistant to any group activity—Alma, Norma, Debra. I relish their pleasure as they eat up the fatty, iron-rich appetizer I am certain these three scrawny women could use. The trio promise to come back later when the main course is served.

Woodhouse has several new residents. The year has brought many changes, as far as residents are concerned. The first to go were Toby and Janice, evicted. Then Madeline died. Sarah left on her own accord. Felice, Debra, and Alma would receive ultimatums, and later they would be shown the door. Denise may be back; for now, she has checked into a therapeutic community for help in sobering up.

Before she left, Denise described the TC. "It looks like a Jack Lalanne's and the tables have white tablecloths and real silverware, can you imagine that?"

Helen Samowitz is one of the new women. The first time
I meet her, Nora brings her by and introduces us. "Look at
these!" Nora exclaims as Helen and I exchange pleasantries.
She's found a box full of donated shoes and tries on a pair of
spike heels. They don't quite go with her sweats and T-shirt,
but Nora's strong legs look great in pumps. Dixie, who's in
charge of the "clothing department," looks on.

Helen examines a donated Krups electric drip coffee pot.
She is trying to figure out how to put together the different
parts of the machine. It turns out the filter basket someone
threw into the carton does not fit the coffee maker. It takes
some time before any of us solves that mean puzzle. Helen
becomes confused, almost disoriented. Nora and I explain
about the mismatch with the coffee pot, but Helen insists on
matching the two incongruous pieces.

Nora chooses six pair of shoes, and Dixie nods her okay
to take them. "They're good for going to church," Nora says.

"Oh," I ask surprised, "you've been going to church?"

"Not yet," Nora answers. "I'm planning to go soon."

Helen's story sounds familiar. The forty-year-old woman
looks more like seventy. It is difficult to imagine that she has
young children. There are four of them, ranging in age from
six years to nineteen. Like Helen, her husband, Reginald, is
"homeless." The children are in foster care.

"I will not allow my children to be adopted," Helen snaps
defensively, as if one too many people has asked her to place
them. "They are *my* children. My husband and I love our
children and want to care for them." She says the oldest
child, a boy, was conceived during a rape.

Helen says that, one time, she was thrown out of a fifth-
floor window by a man. That's why she walks with a bad
limp and lost her voicebox. Helen has a pin in her leg and an
artificial voicebox in her throat. To speak, Helen presses a

hole in her neck. "God's angels are looking over me," Helen remarks of her survival.

Helen likes to talk about her husband, although word has it he is persona non grata at Woodhouse. In the few short weeks she's been at Woodhouse, Helen's husband has already threatened her and harassed some of the other women. "He uses the stage name of James Brown Jr.," Helen proudly tell us, "'cause he's a singer and dancer."

"He does look like James Brown," Nora agrees, "I've seen him."

Nora adds, "But he looks *mean.*"

"He looks mean, but he's not mean," Helen assures her. "They don't want me to see him because they worry since he has a temper. I know he has a temper, but I know how to handle him."

"He's had a brain stroke," Helen says. Her husband lives in a Bronx shelter. "From crack, but he doesn't do that anymore," she explains in a creaky voice. Helen says Reginald was lured into crack use by a young woman who came to live with the couple in their dilapidated Bronx apartment. She stayed for three years, until Reginald threw her out. "He found 'cum' stains in the bed—she was fucking some other guy because of crack."

Now, Reginald has "some kind of disease from this girl," but Helen doesn't know what it is. All she knows is he won't have sex with her anymore because "he doesn't want me to get sick too."

I AM WORKING in the kitchen as other women wander in to chat among themselves at the table. I find it nearly impossible to prepare a meal in an unstocked kitchen, and my frustration shows as I clatter around searching for this tool or that. Although I can borrow almost anything I need from Lenore's house kitchen downstairs, it's a bother to constantly run up and down each time I remember some item I need—a potholder, olive oil, a ladle, pepper, a baster, a platter.

In the meantime, I don't want to miss the conversation among the women gathering at the table.

Hattie is complaining about Alma. She has had her fill of trouble with Alma, especially since the two women live across from each other. "Alma always comes in late—two, three, four in the morning. She slams her door. She slams the bathroom door too. She's always waking me up. So I talked to her about it. I asked her, 'Alma, is it that you don't like me because I'm white?' I mean, I am the only white person on my entire floor. And Alma insulted me. She said, 'You're not white, you're mixed.' I said, 'If I were mixed, wouldn't I admit it? What kind of a person do you think I am who would deny that she is mixed if she were mixed?'" Hattie continues, "I'm Polish and German and English. That's who I am, and that's what I told Alma. What kind of terrible person does she think I am if I pretended to be white if I was really mixed?"

"Alma's always taking Linda's money for drugs," Hattie points out to the others. "I hear her all the time. Linda's always asking Alma to go to the store for her for cigarettes or whatever, and Alma comes back and says, 'Sorry, I lost the money,' or 'Sorry, I bought the cigarettes but the man in the store never gave me change back.' It makes me mad at Linda 'cause Linda's always doing this with Alma. She knows Alma has a bad habit, and Linda's always giving Alma her money and then losing it. She doesn't learn her lesson. Makes me wanted to punch Linda in the face."

"You know how it is," Diane answers. "Stealing's a big problem around here, things walk out of here."

T HAT'S WHAT the women always say when I suggest we find a way to fill the little kitchen with basic supplies. It'll never work, they tell me. We can get donations, buy things, even try to lock them up. They'll still "walk out of here."

Diane continues, "Remember the time someone stole a bag of clothes from Dixie?" Dixie, in charge of distributing clothing donations that come to the house, reported the theft a few weeks ago. Dixie nods in disgust.

It seems Alma went a little too far this time. Over the weekend, Linda Williams received word that her sister had died. While Linda had gone to see about her dead sister, Alma somehow ended up in her neighbor's room. They say Alma stole twenty dollars from Linda.

"How come she keep doing things like that?" Hattie wants to know why Linda lets Alma *in* her room. "She's always giving Alma cigarettes, always answering her door to Alma in the middle of the night, and that bothers other people on the floor too."

Dresden takes the floor. "I don't mean to interrupt," she says, "but I think Linda has gotten better on this. Don't forget, this time Linda actually accused Alma of stealing the money, something she never would have done in the past. Think about it. She reported that her money was stolen. She's come a long way."

Dresden is Woodhouse's best activist, although her efforts don't always have long-term results. She's the one who organized Woodhouse's monthly "community meetings" in which tenants discuss pressing issues and try to find solutions.

Since its inception, the central issue for the community group has been harassment. Harassment, Dixie explains, is "women harassing other women for money or cigarettes. It's not about if someone asks you for a cigarette, and you know it's just that they're short and that you'll get it back from them. It's the ones that ask and ask and ask and they never return anything. Some people get picked on more than others. People know that if I says no it means no."

Dresden's idea is to facilitate dialogue between the harassers and harassed, help people better understand what they are doing to other people, and help the more intimidated women assert themselves. She is confident the meetings spurred Linda to speak up on this latest incident. Even if Linda is not yet able to shut the door on her harassers, she did report the theft of her money and point to Alma as the culprit.

Dresden's idea is designed as an alternative to the customary "punitive" approach: eviction or the threat of eviction.

Just then, Sol Revilla strolls into the library, wide-eyed again. The discussion comes to an abrupt halt. "I love white people, and I hope they never die," she announces. "Besides, they have better hair than we do."

I DECIDE TO pick up a few things for the kitchen and look for Nora at the same time. The past couple of days, Nora has been on the run, out of the house again. I turn the corner of Amsterdam Avenue and see Nora looking around nervously. She shifts from one leg to the other as she fingers the rosary beads wrapped tightly around her wrist.

We hold onto each other for a long time until Nora breaks our embrace with her familiar apologies. "I'm sorry, I'm so sorry," she cries, "please forgive me."

"Stop it," I plead, reminding her again I'm not the one who needs to forgive her. "I'm glad to see you're okay."

"Marvin gave me an ultimatum." Nora fills me in. "I had another outburst, a fight with Tanya, and I called her a crippled bitch. Any more outbursts, I have to leave. They say the other ladies are afraid of me and I cannot do this anymore. I'm terrified. I can't lose my home.

"Marvin gave me advice. He says I should walk away when my anger comes over me, when I'm on the verge of an outburst. I don't have a choice. One more outburst and I'm out. Like Alma's gonna be–she's gonna be gone now too.

"Marvin made me sign a paper. It says I understand that this is my last chance. They say my outbursts are a direct violation of my lease."

I don't get what happened, what happens. Nora helps me understand.

"I got a phone call. It was from a psychiatrist. He said my mother is in a psychiatric hospital and I should come see her. I told him I can't. I told him I can't do that, I have too many problems with my mother. After that, I felt bad. All I know is, that night, I was out the door.

"But, you know, I always come back. One time, when I was still living on the street, homeless, I met Mr. Linton from the Volunteers of America. And he always said, 'You're gonna be the one that's gonna get out of this. Something about you, Nora.' 'Cause I was always fighting. I was always trying. I was always getting clean for a couple of months, and then I'd fall back. I would always relapse. But he would always say, 'Nora, keep trying.' He's the one who took me in a van to Montrose. He took me to rehab because I was a vet."

"I was in rehab. It was in the middle of my Forty-second Street thing, on the Deuce, into crack and alcohol. The people in the rehab said you have to send for one of your parents. 'Miss Gaines, can you get a hold of your mother?' I said, 'Sure, I'll get a hold of my mother.' My mother probably thought I was sick or something like that, so she came up to the hospital. My mother came up to the hospital, but I was in the rehab. I was on the rehab floor.

"This is where the parent and the daughter sit down. The social workers or the counselors, they want to see how you interrelate with your mother, or your mother interrelates with you, and what is going on between the two or whatever like that.

"The social worker said, 'Mrs. Gaines, do you know why your daughter is here?'

"My mother said, 'Yeah, they told me she has pneumonia.'

"And I said, *'What?'* I said, 'I'm not here for no pneumonia. I'm here for drinkin' and druggin'.'

The social worker says, 'Mrs. Gaines, do you know why your daughter drinks and drugs?' And then she says, 'Nora, tell your mother why it is you feel you are drinkin' and druggin'. What are the feelings that come up when you're drinkin' and druggin'? Talk to your mother.'

I started to say, 'Mommy, a lot of times I remember when I was little you used to come to us, you used to take us down to the park and sit with us on a bench at two or three in the morning. And Mommy, that used to bother me—it used to scare me. And why, Mommy, did we used to sometimes have to live in darkness—you used to turn out all the lights and we used to have to walk around in the dark, darkness and candles. It used to bother me a lot because it used to scare me. And I want to know why, why Mommy, why you and dad used to always fight a lot, why he always hit you a lot, and you used to always cry. And I wanted to know why when he used to beat me you wouldn't come in there and hold me and hug me and tell me everything is going to be okay and you was going to get rid of him and call the police and stuff like that?'

"Well, I wasn't even half way into it when she stopped me and she said, 'Nora, the Bible says you're not supposed to use drugs and you're not supposed to drink.' Mind you now, the counselor says, 'Mrs. Gaines, she wants to know why–Do you have any answers for her?–talk to your daughter, Mrs. Gaines, talk to her, she needs you to talk to her.'

"'I have nothing more to say.' She gets up. 'I have nothing more to say about this. Nora, the Bible says we are not supposed to drink and drug and that's all I have to say. I have no more to say to you. You, Nora, get yourself straightened out,' and she left. My mother's like that. To this day, she's like that.

"My mother gets me upset. She just makes me angry. I can't look at my mother and dissect this and say this is what's wrong with her, this is why she's doing this, and this and that. Only a psychiatrist can do that. My mother needs to see a psychiatrist very badly. I can't tell her that what she's doing, that this type of behavior is wrong, is sick in some way.

"I told her, 'You have a lot of good stuff in you, Mommy, but you also have a lot of evil, sick stuff in you that you did when we were little.' And I don't want all that fear, you know, she put a lot fear in us about people, always telling us people are gonna do this to you, people are gonna do that to you; watch out, somebody dropped that for you, if you step in it you're gonna be cursed and all this stuff like that. She put a lot of sick stuff in us. And I don't want this woman coming around again to me now that I'm trying to get healthy.

"It's frustrating. But I'm not gonna be totally frustrated from her 'cause I'm forty-four years old and know what I say? The hell–I love my mother–but you know what? The hell with her sick stuff. I do not allow myself to be *totally* frustrated."

"What about when you were homeless. Did she know?" I ask Nora.

"She didn't know."

"What did she think you were doing?"

"She didn't know, but she was getting my mail. I made

her my payee, and she cashed my checks. My mother would
tell me to meet her at Lincoln Center to pick up my money.
I would have to go in the bathroom and wash up and find
clean clothes from somewhere because my mother was
like middle class. She comes from a middle-class family
background.

"One time I went up there to Lincoln Center. I was dressed
neatly and clean. But my hair was short, because I lost all
my hair due to using and drinking and not eating.

"She took one look at me, her face dropped. She brought
me $750 dollars. She gave it to me. She looked at me and
said, 'Nora, I did not bring you up in this world to use drugs.'
She knew right away what I was doing. 'Look at you, what
happened to your hair?' She was very disappointed. And for
the second time she says, 'You get yourself straightened out,
Nora. I don't know what it is you're doing, but you better get
yourself straightened out.'

"I jumped in a cab right outside of Lincoln Center, a Yellow cab, and I went straight to beat myself up bad. My heart
started to give out on me at some points because I used the
whole money on drinkin' and druggin' and my friends in
abandoned buildings, just crackin' it up, going crazy, and
everything else.

"At this point now, I'm sleeping in an abandoned car, in
a lot. Sick as a dog. I'm spittin' up. Sometimes I caught pneumonia. I would go out in the street, down by the Javitz Con-
vention, on that block. I would go out to wash up, and I'd go
back to sleep in the parking lot. And I was sick as a dog.

"So I had taken the money and I came back. I smoked it
up, I drank it up, I gave the money out to people and friends.
I wound up with jaundice, I wound up with hepatitis. The
people there, they touched my forehead. 'She's burning up,'
and they called the police. They had to put me in the hospital, which I got a touch of cirrhosis.

"I left the hospital. I went back to the Port, but I always ended up with fevers. There was one time I was so sick with a fever, I had to stay in an exit. This guy told me to sleep on his spot. He was sick too. And we're dying, man, we were like the walking dead. He told me, 'Nora, sleep here.' And I slept there for two days, and a police came down and says, 'What are you doing here?' I said, 'Officer, I am very sick. I had a fever for two days and I can't walk or nothing.' He was nice enough. He says, 'Okay, stay there, get some rest.' And he left me there.

"Another guy came back with food and soup. They would smoke right there on the steps, but I couldn't smoke I was so sick. There would be people saying, 'Where could we go to smoke?' I ain't never seen these people, they're smoking crack. We had business people smoke crack. I didn't believe it! They would bring them to the exit and sittin 'em down with their briefcases, 'Here, here I gotta stem, here. Go on man, enjoy yourself, nobody gonna mess with you here.' And the guy would say, 'Where can we get some more?' And he pick up his briefcase. People, guys that I thought would never use crack.

"I was shocked. I was shocked by all the people use crack. 'Cause you get the stereotype that only Puerto Ricans and black people use crack, and that's not so. Here I had people walk up to me. They'd be in the best hotels and smoke crack.

"Now I'm thinking about what I can do now. I'm thinking of getting into acting and maybe taking some acting classes. My psychiatrist told me he feels as though I should go into the theater, you know? That's a psychiatrist's point of view of my personality. That's what he suggested. But I don't know what the hell I want to do. Maybe I can help with, get involved in positive things outside of Woodhouse.

"I wouldn't mind one day writing a story about a girl. I mean writing a story about a woman based on all the stuff she went through from childhood to alcoholism and drug addiction to sobriety. The good and the bad in my life, but it doesn't have to be my life. There's a lot of people out here who went through the same stuff. There are similarities, you know? People could identify with a lot of this stuff–how I'm trying to stay sober and still being faced with a lot of walls, and being aware of a lot that has been done. It would be about my path to recovery, and I'll call it *From Hell to Heaven.*

"I'm thinking that maybe one day, somebody would pick it up and read it."

I AM SCRUBBING the kitchen when Milagros Rojas comes in to watch. Milagros has just moved in. This is the first time we've had a chance to meet. The kitchen has become so dirty, I can't stand it anymore. Armed with Fantastik and Soft Scrub, I set out to "do a thorough cleaning," just as my father taught me years ago.

Milagros is confused. I introduce myself and tell her what, in general, I do at Woodhouse. Research and writing, except, of course, for today. Today, I'm cleaning.

Milagros stares wide-eyed and decides I am a student. She wants to know if I have a family. She wants to know if I have a husband, children, a kitchen of my own.

I show her photographs of my two kids. First, Milagros studies the picture of the boy. "He helps you, right," Milagros doesn't ask, but declares (How does she know?). Glancing at the second picture, she says, 'Your daughter, she's not so easy, she's spirited." (How can she tell from this sweet little school photo?).

I turn back to my chore, eager to have the kitchen spotless before the cooking group begins for the day. Milagros continues to watch me. I wonder if she thinks I'm doing a good job, or what.

Suddenly, Milagros turns to leave, chanting maniacally, "The kitchen is filthy. The bathrooms are dirty too. They clean them with dirty sponges. Dirt and filth, it's everywhere. It's disgusting. The bathrooms are filthy, the toilets, even the tubs are dirty." As Milagros walks down the hallway, her shouts become a mutter.

By now, the cooking group is in full swing and the library is crowded. It will be the last time I share in the cooking at Woodhouse. Crystal shows Helen how to whip eggs for Spanish omelets. Nora and I chop onions and green pepper, sharing a chair at the table. Helen struggles with the eggs until Susan finally takes over for her. We are snacking on a box of matzos I've brought to the group.

Crystal's in a great mood today. Her youngest boy, Davey, has been moved from foster care to his father's house. That means Crystal will be seeing more of her little boy. "He is my heart." Crystal smiles as she putters around the kitchen, "I love him, I love him, I love him, I love him, I love him."

"I might be seeing my son too," Dixie says offhandedly.

"Your son?" I ask, straining my memory. I didn't think Dixie had any children.

"My son, Paul," Dixie answers. "He's twenty-two and in the military."

"Dixie, I didn't know you had a son."

"I know," she tells me. "I do. I just never talked about it before. I kept it to myself. My aunts gave me a picture of him with his fiance. He's wearing his military uniform, and he looks so handsome. I kept it to myself. I didn't want to get into the whole thing, talking about it. Since I've been in touch with my aunts, they've been telling me about him. They gave me this picture. Now I want to show it to everyone. The proud mother, I guess." Dixie brings out the photograph.

"He looks so much like you, especially the eyes," I say. "He looks sweet and nice."

"He looks exactly like his father," Dixie smiles at the photo. "I wrote to him about six weeks ago. It was a short note and I kept it light. I didn't want to get into anything too heavy. I don't know how much he knows about me. I think he knows what his father has told him about me, that I'm 'sick.' He's very close to his father. He's in the Marines, in California, but he comes to New York once in awhile, to visit his father. He visits my aunts in Brooklyn too.

"When his father and I divorced, Paul didn't want to leave the house he'd been raised in. I gave his father custody, no fight. I could have visited him, but I couldn't handle it."

Dixie and I hold hands across the table. I rest my hands on Dixie's thin arms, then stroke her, "I hope he writes back."

"I hope so too," is all she can say.

On my way out, Milagros catches me at the front door. "Don't forget us," she warns, "You better come back and don't forget us. Otherwise, you will be *lost*."

Notes

Prologue

1. While New York's Rudolph Giuliani and other city mayors proudly announce the success of welfare reform, hunger in America is on the rise (Lieberman 1998; Roberts and Roberts 1998; "Use of Soup Kitchens" 1998; Sarasohn 1997; New York City Coalition against Hunger 1997); a shocking number of American children are living in poverty (Annie E. Casey Foundation 1998; Kilborn 1996); and work and income opportunities for the poor and working class are decreasing while economic pressures mount (Waterston 1998; Greenhouse 1998; Finder 1998; Hernandez 1998b; Conniff 1998; Carter 1998; Green 1997; Lazere 1997; Leete and Bania 1997; Krueger, Accles, and Wernick 1997).

2. Built on a project designed by research psychiatrist Ezra Susser, my ethnographic research, which extended from 1994 to 1996, was used as a first step in a larger effort to develop an HIV prevention program for a population that has been identified as at high risk for infection. The overall aim was to identify specific determinants of sexual risk behavior and barriers to risk reduction for these women in the hopes of developing an HIV prevention curriculum that is relevant to their actual situation. This research was supported by a Center Grant from NIMH to the HIV Center for Clinical and Behavioral Research #P50-MH43520 and by NIMH-supported training grant #5T32-MH19139, Behavioral Sciences Research Training in HIV Infection Program. My association with the HIV Center coincided with the early developments of an AIDS prevention research project focused on "homeless, mentally ill women." In their work

with "homeless, mentally ill men," Ezra Susser, M.D., Ph.D., and his team had earlier studied the determinants of risk behaviors among residents of a men's shelter in New York City. The team went on to conduct research on the developing, testing, and applications of an intervention for the men. In turning their attention to women, Susser et al. developed a research strategy in which exploratory, "elicitation" research constituted the early stages. My role on the study centered on this aspect of the larger project. As principal investigator of the study, Susser chose Woodhouse as the site of the research, arranging my entree and gaining the consent for me to conduct qualitative research there (PI IRB #2328).

3. This book is based on my more than twenty years of study of, and deep concern about, urban poverty in the United States. An academically trained anthropologist, I began studying the consequences of poverty as a day care teacher in a poor neighborhood in Brooklyn. I had early on learned about peasantry, fascism, patriarchy, dictatorship, migration, transnationalism, revolution, and diaspora from parents who experienced these things over this century. The lens through which I view the world has also, in part, been shaped by my having experienced enormous monetary downs and ups and a profound sense of loss and financial insecurity as a child growing up between New York, Cuba, and Puerto Rico; at the same time, I was encouraged to become upwardly mobile and to develop an identifiably "American middle-class" personal style and mode of presentation. At this moment, I fit into the category of the financially comfortable—a married, white-American-Jewish-mother raising two children in the suburbs of New York City.

4. Frances Fox Piven made these remarks as a discussant in the invited session "Gender, Class, and History in the City: A Dialogue with Dolores Hayden and Frances Fox Piven" at the 1997 annual meeting of the American Anthropological Society in Washington, D.C.

5. I draw the term *dustbin* from Frederick Cooper and Ann Stoler, quoted by Jane Schneider in *Articulating Hidden Histories: Exploring the Influence of Eric R. Wolf*:

> Europeans, the first carriers of capitalist forces . . . sought to legitimate their expanding power by installing a dynamic of distinctions. Some subordinate groups came to be identified, named, and classified as welcome participants in the wider system, whereas other groups were stigmatized—consigned in the apt phrase of Frederick Cooper and Ann Stoler, to the "dustbin of backwardness." "In the

capitalist mode," Wolf writes, "the regnant ideology assumes the equality of all participants in the market, in the face of basic distinctions in political and economic power." Capitalist ideology links these distinctions to differences of "virtue and merit." To take one example, participation in capitalist culture generally brings with it the "ability to acquire valued commodities"; conversely, "inability to consume signals social defeat." The rhythm of labor mobilization and abandonment "continuously reproduces an opposition between virtuous consumers and the disvalued poor."

Chapter 1

1. By some estimates, Woodhouse is one of more than fifty housing facilities located in District 7 (Goldberg 1994:40). Among these facilities are SROs (single-room occupancy residences, private or not-for-profit), transitional housing, and community residences. The surge in the number and variety of housing facilities coincided with the emergence of homelessness as a *visible* "social problem" over the past twenty years (Stern 1984; Blau 1992).

2. Most of the nearly fifty Woodhouse "beds" are designated according to the New York/New York (New York City/New York State) agreement, which structures housing for "homeless, mentally ill" individuals. The New York/New York agreement, which expired in the fall of 1997 "after [New York state governor] Pataki and his fellow Republicans in the Senate refused to refinance it," was renewed in the 1998 New York State budget and is now known as the New York–New York II agreement (Hernandez 1998a; Kennedy 1997).

3. Since the early 1980s, there has been much debate about the number of homeless in America and how to measure their numbers (Jencks 1994a, b). In one recent study, the prevalence of "lifetime literal homelessness," defined as "sleeping in shelters, abandoned buildings, bus and train stations, etc." was 13.5 million people–7.4 percent of the U.S. population. The study's authors report the prevalence of five-year literal homelessness for the years 1985 to 1990 at 3.1 percent–5.7 million people (Link et al. 1994: 1907). Another estimate puts the number of homeless in the United States at between 600,000 to 3 million people, the majority located in central cities (Tynes et al. 1993:276). Passaro cites New York City Department of Planning data for 1990 that report 33,156 homeless adults in Manhattan (1996:19). By 1991, according to Dehavenon, nearly 6,000 families were staying in New York City's shelter sys-

tem, and by 1997, 300,000 poor families live "doubled up," rendering their homelessness invisible (Dehavenon 1997:10–11; 1996: 51–53).

4. To be approved for housing placement at Woodhouse, candidates must apply to the New York City Human Resources Administration. The application, completed and submitted by a case manager or social worker, includes social, medical, and psychiatric assessments. Among other requirements, applicants must document their "homelessness" either by having used a municipal shelter in fourteen of the last sixty days or by submitting an "identifying letter" from a reliable source, such as a drop-in center, outreach program or the Partnership for the Homeless (Coalition for the Homeless 1993). During the 1980s, 350 Lafayette had served as one such central intake point.

5. In a review of the literature on "the homeless mentally ill," Tynes et al. conclude: "Approximately, 30%–40% evince major psychiatric disorders, such as schizophrenia or bipolar disorder, while more than 60% may be alcoholics and more than 25% abuse drugs. Additionally, research shows that 10%–20% of the homeless carry a dual diagnosis of severe mental illness and substance abuse disorders" (1993:276; see also Coalition for the Homeless 1993). Woodhouse, licensed and, in part, funded by the New York State Office of Mental Health, opened its doors in the late 1980s. Its clients rank among those tabulated in the statistics above. A majority of Woodhouse residents have been diagnosed with schizophrenia, major depression, or bipolar disorder–Axis I disorders, according to the DSM-III-R diagnostic system (American Psychiatric Association 1998). Between 90 and 95 percent of the women are prescribed psychiatric medications, and, according to clinical staff, nearly all (95 percent) take their medications.

6. The portraits I present also call attention to what Gilman refers to as "the banality of real mental illness" (1988:12–13).

7. Antipsychotic medications most commonly prescribed to Woodhouse women are the standard neuroleptics: Haldol, Stelazine, Mellaril, Prolixin, and Thorazine. Side effects that often result from drug treatment may require further medication. Most common side effects are akathisia (restlessness, agitation, anxiety) and tardive dyskinesia (involuntary, tic-like movements) (Burwell-Sipes 1993). Those who suffer these effects are given anti-Parkinsonian agents like Artane or Cogentin. More recently, some women have

been prescribed Risperidone and Clozapine, newer antipsychotic drugs which have fewer side effects than the standard neuroleptics. At Woodhouse, other clients receive Prozac (an antidepressant), lithium (a psychostimulant for bipolar disorder or schizoaffective disorder) and Buspar (an antianxiety medication) (Burwell-Sipes 1993; Estroff 1981).

8. Passaro cites "the massive defunding of federal housing that took place in the 1980s, [an] astounding 80% decrease, from $30 billion in 1980 to $6 billion in 1990," as an important aspect of "the economic basis of homelessness today" (1996:22; see also Stone 1993:126–62; Schussheim 1987).

9. See Baxter and Hopper 1981; Hopper, Susser and Conover 1986; Hopper 1988; Williams 1988, 1996; Barak 1991; Sassen 1991; Stone 1993; Smith 1996 on gentrification and displacement in U.S. cities during the 1980s.

10. The women who live in Woodhouse receive Supplemental Security Income (SSI), monthly payments provided to disabled people with limited income and resources (Department of Health and Human Services 1994). During 1994 and 1995, the average annual income from SSI to a Woodhouse resident was $10,500, according to the clinical director. As a tenant of Woodhouse, each resident signs a rental agreement stipulating the cost of room, board, and additional services. These costs represent approximately 75 percent of the SSI income, the remainder going to the resident as "personal allowance." A typical service agreement stipulates the tenant pay Woodhouse, per month, $275 in rent and $388 for additional services. Included among these services are "three meals a day, heat as required by law, hot and cold water for bathroom, and linen service and laundry facilities." Residents' income from SSI is managed by the supervising agency, which also distributes allowances to the women. On average, the women receive allowances of $210 per month, portioned out twice weekly on special "banking days."

Chapter 2

1. During the course of the research, residents moved in and out of Woodhouse, somewhat changing its demographic composition. Counts taken from resident lists at various times over the two-year research period show that approximately 65–70 percent of residents are African American, 25 percent white, and the remainder

either Latina or Asian. The women are primarily from poor or working-class families and range in age from their mid-twenties to early seventies (with most between thirty and fifty years old). At any given time, there are approximately 25–30 percent mental illness/chemical addiction (MICA) clients, residents diagnosed with "mental illness and chemical addictions."

2. Woodhouse has a clinical and operations staff. Case managers, each with a caseload of ten to twelve women, work most closely with the residents. Included among the case managers is a MICA coordinator. The program manager supervises the operations staff, which includes four security guards and receptionists (security and reception are generally the same person), maintenance staff, and three cooks. Support staff include an administrative assistant and a fiscal clerk. Volunteers at Woodhouse include a psychiatrist and student interns from various city graduate schools of social work. Staff turnover is highest for case managers and security guards/receptionists, although between 1995 and 1997, there have been two new clinical directors and program managers at Woodhouse.

3. In the early 1990s, Woodhouse was cited by the New York State Office of Mental Health as a model of "alternative housing for mentally-ill homeless adults." Some might argue that Woodhouse self-selects the more compliant and agreeable among potential residents, making its success more easily achieved, while leaving the more difficult cases to the streets or city shelters.

4. Woodhouse also offers "individual client counseling sessions, a program for dually-diagnosed mentally-ill and chemically-addicted (MICA) clients; in-house medication monitoring; a full-time activities schedule; and an in-house pre-vocational work program."

5. The Coalition for the Homeless reports that "a woman who becomes homeless is likely to be raped within one week after she loses her housing" (1994:2). According to Bureau of Justice statistics on the incidence of rape in the United States, aggregate data for the years 1979–87 show there were 1.39 million female victims of completed and attempted rape in the United States (Maguire and Flanagan 1991:271). More recent Department of Justice statistics, gathered by use of a new, redesigned methodology, show that in 1992 and 1993, women ages twelve or older annually report 500,000 rapes and sexual assaults in the United States (Bachman and Saltzman 1993).

Chapter 3

1. Although the American public decries "violent or criminal abuse of guns," the wholesale and retail gun industries benefit from the sale and distribution of their products to any gun consumer, including those in the lucrative informal sector of the drug industry (Wright 1995; Williams 1989; Waterston 1993). In the United States, 2.3 million handguns were produced in 1980. By 1991, the production of handguns had dropped to 1.8 million as manufacturers began to add assault weapons and high-capacity pistols to their product lines (Sugarmann: 1993, N/d).

2. Recent figures on recruitment advertising show that Congress increased recruiting resources for the armed services by $89 million in 1995 and by $31 million in 1996 (Pang 1996). For the years 1980–82, blacks made up 29 percent of the total Department of Defense manpower (U.S. Bureau of the Census 1996:360). According to Fred Pang, assistant secretary of defense for force management policy, "minority" representation in the armed forces stands at approximately 30 percent (1996).

Chapter 4

1. The loss of manufacturing jobs and rise in the service industry over the past thirty years in the United States is well documented (Sassen 1991, 1996b; Harvey 1989). Figures for New York City show that manufacturing employment dropped by 46 percent between 1979 and 1994, representing a loss of some 245,000 manufacturing jobs (O'Neill, Garcia, and McCormick 1997: 17-18). A surge in the better-paying, higher-skilled jobs associated with the new growth industries has left the less skilled and less educated out of the advancement loop.

2. Several Woodhouse women earn a little extra money in the in-house work program which Victoria explained helps "get their feet wet and get them back into the mainstream." Managed by one of the case managers, the work program provides participants ten to fifteen hours of work per week. Positions in the work program include receptionist, kitchen aide, librarian, housekeeper, and office worker, and all jobs pay a dollar per hour. Under the eligibility requirements for SSI, the first $65 of earnings received in a month does not count in figuring SSI; therefore monies women earn in the work program do not exceed the allowable limit. Countable income, as defined by SSI, would be subtracted from the SSI

federal benefit rate. If such income exceeded the allowable limit, SSI benefits would be stopped (Department of Health and Human Services 1994).

Chapter 5

1. On the basis of staff estimates and residents' self-reports, 2 to 9 percent of residents were HIV positive. The range in this estimate is based on changes in resident composition over time, not on differing accounts by staff and residents. The 2 percent estimate reflects the number of HIV positive residents who remained after others had moved out.

2. In the American mind," writes Doug Henwood, "poor and black are synonymous," despite the fact that "almost half–48 percent–of the poor are non-Hispanic whites" (1997:177, 183). Susan is among those who are poor and white. Ethnic minorities are, however, disproportionately represented among the poor in the United States. Data from 1993 show the poverty rate for each of the three main ethnic groups as follows: 33 percent blacks, 31 percent Hispanics, 10 percent whites (Henwood 1997:183).

Chapter 6

1. Recent statistics show that in the United States, AIDS is now spreading at a faster rate among women than among men. For example, Beth E. Schneider and Nancy E. Stoller report that AIDS cases increased 29 percent among women compared to 18 percent among men in 1990, and 151 percent among women compared to 105 percent among men in 1993 (1995:7). According to the Centers for Disease Control (CDC), the fourth leading cause of death in 1993 among American women twenty-five to forty-four years of age was HIV infection (1995b:2). Importantly, HIV infection in 1993 was the leading cause of death among black women and the third leading cause of death among Latina women in this age group (CDC 1995b:2). Put another way, by the mid 1990s, nearly three-fourths (73 percent) of women with AIDS in the United States are black or Latina (Freudenberg and Zimmerman 1995:1). Data through 1997 show more than three-fourths (76 percent) of women with AIDS in the United States are black or Latina (CDC 1997). For the most part, women have become infected by their sexual partners (Doyal 1995; CDC 1994, 1997). Anke A. Ehrhardt and colleagues translate these data to estimate that, in 1992, approximately 80,000 women of childbearing age were infected with HIV

(1992:38). For the years 1989–1992, the CDC reports that 7,000 HIV-infected women gave birth each year to 1,000–2,000 HIV-infected infants (1995b:3). According to Schneider and Stoller, "For every HIV-infected child left orphaned by HIV, 2 or 3 other uninfected children will also be orphaned. There will be an estimated 25,000 young children and 21,000 adolescents orphaned by AIDS in 1995; 75,000 AIDS orphans are projected by the year 2000. So far, no public policy addresses this issue" (1995:314; see also Farmer, Connors, and Simmons 1996).

Chapter 9

1. Indeed, in a 1998 *New York Times* article headlined "Prisons Replace Hospitals for the Nation's Mentally Ill," it is noted, "On any given day, almost 200,000 people behind bars are known to suffer from the three most severe mental illnesses," and "homeless people are charged with minor crimes that are byproducts of their illnesses; others are picked up with no charges at all, in what police call mercy arrests, simply for acting strange" (Butterfield 1998a).

2. News items about recent research on violence and the mentally ill report that "the studies found that mental patients . . . are no more violent than other members of their community, unless they have been abusing alcohol or drugs" (Butterfield 1998b). According to one psychiatric researcher quoted, mental illness is a much smaller risk factor for violence than is "being young, male, poor or addicted to alcohol or drugs"; despite these findings, the *New York Times* chose the following headline for its report on the study: "Studies of Mental Illness Show Links to Violence"–wording that only reinforces false popular perceptions and furthers stigmatization of the mentally ill (Butterfield 1998b; Steadman et al. 1998).

Chapter 11

1. A recent study in Boston published in the *Annals of Internal Medicine* reports that AIDS was the leading cause of death among homeless women and men ages twenty-five to forty-four years old; the average age at death was forty-seven (Hwang, Orav, and O'Connell 1997).

References

Aaronson, Stephanie, and Stephen V. Cameron. 1997. *Poverty in New York City 1996: An Update and Perspectives.* New York: Community Service Society (June).

Abercrombie, Nicholas, and Bryan S. Turner. 1982. "The Dominant Ideology Thesis." In *Classes, Power, and Conflict: Classical and Contemporary Debates,* ed. Anthony Giddens and David Held. Berkeley: University of California Press.

Agar, Michael H. 1996 (1980). *The Professional Stranger: An Informal Introduction to Ethnography.* 2d ed. New York: Academic.

Allen D. M., J. S. Lehman, T. A. Green, M. L. Lindegren, I. M. Onorato, and W. Forrester. 1995. "HIV Infection among Homeless Adults and Runaway Youth, United States, 1989–1992." AIDS 8: 1593–98.

American Psychiatric Association. 1987. *Diagnostic and Statistical Manual of Mental Disorders.* 3d ed. Washington, D.C.: American Psychiatric Association.

Ami, Ash. 1994. *Post-Fordism: A Reader.* Cambridge, Mass.: Blackwell.

Annie E. Casey Foundation. 1998. *Kids Count Data Book.* Baltimore: Annie E. Casey Foundation. .

Aschenbrenner, Joyce. 1975. *Lifelines.* New York: Rinehart and Winston.

Ayuso Mateos J. L., F. Montanes, I. Lastra, S. Plaza, and J. Pacazo de la Garza. 1994. "HIV Seroprevalence in an Acute Psychiatric Unit." AIDS Impact: Biopsychosocial Aspects of HIV Infection. 2d International Conference. Brighton, U.K.

215

Bachman, Ronet, and Linda E. Saltzman. 1995. *Violence against Women: Estimates from the Redesigned Survey.* U.S. Department of Justice, Bureau of Justice Statistics. Washington, D.C.: USGPO.

Baer, Hans A., Merrill Singer, and Ida Susser. 1997. *Medical Anthropology and the World System: A Critical Perspective.* Westport, Conn.: Bergin and Garvey.

Barak, Gregg. 1991. *Gimme Shelter: A Social History of Homelessness in Contemporary America.* New York: Praeger.

Baum, Alice S., and Donald W. Burnes. 1993. *A Nation in Denial: The Truth about Homelessness.* Boulder, Colo.: Westview Press.

Baxter, Ellen, and Kim Hopper. 1981. *Private Lives/Public Spaces: Homeless Adults on the Streets of New York City.* New York: Community Service Society.

Becker, Howard S. 1964. *The Other Side: Perspectives on Deviance.* New York: Macmillan.

Behar, Ruth. 1993. *Translated Woman. Crossing the Border with Esperanza.* Boston: Beacon.

Bennett, Tony, Graham Martin, Colin Mercer, and Janet Woollacott. 1981. *Culture, Ideology, and Social Process: A Reader.* London: Open University Press.

Berkman, Alan. 1995. "Prison Health: The Breaking Point." *American Journal of Public Health* 85:1616–18.

Blau, Joel. 1987. *The Homeless of New York: A Case Study in Social Welfare Policy.* D.S.W. Thesis, Columbia University.

———. 1992. *The Visible Poor: Homelessness in the United States.* New York: Oxford University Press.

Blumer, Herbert. 1971. "Social Problems as Collective Behavior." *Social Problems* 18(3):298–306.

Bourdieu, Pierre, and Jean-Claude Passeron. 1990. *Reproduction in Education, Society, and Culture.* 2d ed. London: Sage.

Braverman Harry. 1974. *Labor and Monopoly Capital: The Degradation of Work in the Twentieth Century.* New York: Monthly Review Press.

Brock, Fred. 1998. "The Richer Rich and Where They Live." *New York Times.* April 19, business section.

Burt, Martha R. 1992. *Over the Edge: The Growth of Homelessness in the 1980's.* New York. Russell Sage Foundation.

Burwell-Sipes, Lisa. 1993. *Current Clinical Strategies: Handbook of Psychiatric Drugs.* Newport Beach, Calif.: CCS Publishing.

Butterfield, Fox. 1998a. "Prisons Replace Hospitals for the Nation's Mentally Ill." *New York Times.* March 5.

———. 1998b. "Studies of Mental Illness Show Links to Violence." *New York Times.* May 15.

Carter, Chelsea J. 1998. "Poverty in the Spotlight: Fonda's Remarks a Reminder that U.S. Still Has Many Living Below Poverty Level." *Standard Star,* May 7.

Cassell, Joan. 1996. "The Woman in the Surgeon's Body: Understanding Difference." *American Anthropologist* 98(1):41–53.

Castells, Manuel. 1977. *The Urban Question: A Marxist Approach.* Cambridge: MIT Press.

———. 1978. *The City and the Grass Roots.* Berkeley: University of California Press.

Centers for Disease Control. 1994. *Morbidity and Mortality Weekly Reports.* Vol. 43, August 5.

———. 1995a. *Morbidity and Mortality Weekly Reports.* Vol. 44 (RR-7), July 7.

———. 1995b. "Update: AIDS among Women–United States, 1994." *Morbidity and Mortality Weekly Reports.* 44 (5), February 10.

———. 1997. *HIV/AIDS Surveillance Report.* 9 (2), December.

Clarke, John, Stuart Hall, Tony Jefferson, and Brian Roberts. 1975. "Subcultures, Cultures, and Class: A Theoretical Overview." In *Resistance through Rituals: Youth Subcultures in Postwar Britain,* ed. Stuart Hall and Tony Jefferson. London: Hutchinson.

Coalition for the Homeless. 1993. *What is Government For? The Surge of Homeless Persons with Mental Illness in New York City.* New York: Coalition for the Homeless.

———. 1994. *Anti-violence Project Report.* New York: New York State Division of Criminal Justice.

Collins, Pamela, Nance L. Sohler, and Ezra Susser. 1997. "The Potential for Female-Controlled Methods of HIV Prevention for Women with Mental Illness." *Health Psychologist* 18 (4):9, 20–21.

Collins, Sheila. 1996. *Let Them Eat Ketchup! The Politics of Poverty and Inequality.* New York: Monthly Review Press.

Conniff, Ruth. 1998. "Welfare Miracle or Mirage?" *New York Times.* March 7.

Corin, Ellen. 1990. "Facts and Meanings in Psychiatry: An Anthropological Approach to the Lifeworld of Schizophrenics." *Culture, Medicine, and Psychiatry* 14:153–88.

Cournos, Francine, Maureen Empfield, and Ewald Horwath. 1991. "HIV Seroprevalence among Patients Admitted to Two Psychiatric Hospitals." *American Journal of Psychology* 148:1225–30.

Crapanzano, Vincent. 1990. "An Introduction." *Culture, Medicine, and Psychiatry* 14:145–52.

Crawford, Robert. 1994. "The Boundaries of the Self and the Unhealthy Other: Reflections on Health, Culture, and AIDS." *Social Science and Medicine* 38(10):1347–65.

Dalton, Harlon. 1989. "AIDS in Blackface." *Daedalus* 118(3): 205–27.

Dear, Michael, and Jennifer Wolch. 1987. *Landscapes of Despair: From Deinstitutionalization to Homelessness.* Princeton: Princeton University Press.

De Genio, M., A. Chiesi, F. Pariante, N. Falchi Delitala, E. D'Aloia, and D. Esposti. 1994. "Psychiatric Patients May be Considered a New Population at Risk for HIV Infection." AIDS Impact: Biopsychosoical Aspects of HIV Infection. 2d International Conference. Brighton, UK.

Dehavenon, Anna Lou. 1997. *Charles Dickens Meets Franz Kafka in 1997: How the Giuliani Administration Flouted Court Orders and Abused Homeless Families and Children.* Action Research Project on Hunger, Homelessness, and Family Health (November).

Dehavenon, Anna Lou, ed. 1996. *There's No Place Like Home. Anthropological Perspectives on Housing and Homelessness in the United States.* Westport, Conn.: Bergin and Garvey.

Department of Health and Human Services. 1994. *Understanding SSI.* Washington, D.C.: USGPO.

Derber, Charles. 1995. "The Politics of Triage: The Contract with America's Surplus Populations." *Tikkun* 10:37–88.

di Leonardo, Micaela. 1994. "Gender, Race, and Representation: Neighborhood Shift in New Haven." Paper presented at the annual meeting of the American Anthropological Association, Atlanta.

———. 1996. "Patterns of Culture Wars: Anthropology Is the New Target of the Far-Right Heresy-Hunters." *The Nation,* April 8: 25–29.

di Leonardo, Micaela, ed. 1991. *Gender at the Crossroads of Knowledge.* Berkeley: University of California Press.

Doyal, Lesley. 1995. *What Makes Women Sick: Gender and the Political Economy of Health.* New Brunswick, N.J.: Rutgers University Press.

Ehrenreich, Barbara. 1989. *Fear of Falling: The Inner Life of the Middle Class.* New York: Harper Perennial.

———. 1987. "The New Right Attack on Social Welfare." In *The*

Mean Season: The Attack on the Welfare State, ed. Fred Block, Richard A. Cloward, Barbara Ehrenreich, and Frances Fox Piven. New York: Pantheon.

Ehrhardt, Anke A., Sandra Yingling, Rezi Zawadski, and Maria Martinez-Ramirez. 1992. "Prevention of Heterosexual Transmission of HIV: Barriers for Women." *Journal of Psychology and Human Sexuality* 5 (1, 2):37–67.

Estroff, Sue. 1981. *Making It Crazy.* Berkeley: University of California Press.

Estroff, Sue, and William S. Lachicotte, Linda C. Illingworth, and Anne Johnston. 1991. "Everybody's Got a Little Mental Illness: Accounts of Illness and Self among People with Severe, Persistent Mental Illnesses." *Medical Anthropology Quarterly* 5(4): 331–69.

Farmer, Paul. 1988. "Bad Blood, Spoiled Milk: Bodily Fluids as Moral Barometers in Rural Haiti." *American Ethnologist* 15(1): 62–83.

———. 1992. *AIDS and Accusation: Haiti and Geography of Blame.* Berkeley: University of California Press.

———. 1994. *The Uses of Haiti.* Monroe, Maine: Common Courage Press.

———. 1996. "On Suffering and Structural Violence: A View from Below." *Daedalus* 125(1):261–83.

Farmer, Paul, Margaret Connors, and Janie Simmons, eds. 1996. *Women, Poverty and AIDS. Sex, Drugs and Structural Violence.* Monroe, Maine: Common Courage Press.

Fee, Elizabeth, and Nancy Krieger. 1993. "Understanding AIDS: Historical Interpretations and the Limits of Biomedical Individualism." *American Journal of Public Health* 83(10):1477–86.

———. 1994. *Women's Health, Politics and Power: Essays on Sex/ Gender, Medicine, and Public Health.* Amityville, N.Y.: Baywood.

Finder, Alan. 1998. "Evidence Is Scant that Workfare Leads to Full-Time Jobs." *New York Times.* April 12.

Fischer, Pamela J., Robert E. Drake, and William R. Breakey. 1992. "Mental Health Problems among Homeless Persons: A Review of Epidemiological Research from 1980 to 1990." In *Treating the Homeless Mentally Ill: A Report of the Task Force on the Homeless Mentally Ill,* ed. H. Richard Lamb, Leona L. Bachrach, and Frederick I. Kass. Washington, D.C.: American Psychiatric Association.

Forster, E. M. 1921. *Howards End.* New York: Vintage.

Foster, Thomas. 1995. "Circles of Oppression, Circles of Repression: Etel Adnan's Sitt Marie Rose." *PMLA* 110(1):59–74.

Foucault, Michel. 1965. *Madness and Civilisation.* New York: Random House.

———. 1973. *The Birth of the Clinic: An Archaeology of Medical Perception.* New York: Random House.

———. 1978. *The History of Sexuality.* Vol. 2, *An Introduction.* New York: Random House.

———. 1993. "Space, Power, and Knowledge." In *The Cultural Studies Reader,* ed. Simon During. London: Routledge.

Frankl, Viktor E. 1959. *Man's Search for Meaning.* New York: Simon and Schuster.

Fraser, Nancy. 1993. "Clintonism, Welfare, and the Antisocial Wage: The Emergence of a Neoliberal Political Imaginary." *Rethinking Marxism* 6(1):9–23.

———. 1996. "Reply to Zylan." *Signs* 21(2):531–36.

Fraser, Nancy, and Linda Gordon. 1994. "A Genealogy of Dependency: Tracing a Keyword of the U.S. Welfare State." *Signs* 19(2): 309–36.

Freudenberg, Nicholas, and Marc A. Zimmerman, eds. 1995. *AIDS Prevention in the Community: Lessons from the First Decade.* Washington, D.C.: American Public Health Association.

Gilman, Sander L. 1988. *Disease and Representation: Images of Illness from Madness to AIDS.* Ithaca, N.Y.: Cornell University Press.

Ginsburg, Faye, and Anna Lowenhaupt Tsing, eds. 1990. *Uncertain Terms: Negotiating Gender in American Culture.* Boston: Beacon.

Glasser, Irene. 1994. *Homelessness in Global Perspective.* New York: G. K. Hall.

———. 1988. *More than Bread: Ethnography of a Soup Kitchen.* Tuscaloosa: University of Alabama Press.

Glazer, Nathan, and Daniel P. Moynihan. 1963. *Beyond the Melting Pot: The Negroes, Puerto Ricans, Jews, Italians, and Irish of New York City.* Cambridge: MIT Press and Harvard University Press.

Glick Schiller, Nina. 1992. "What's Wrong with This Picture? The Hegemonic Construction of Culture in AIDS Research in the United States." *Medical Anthropology Quarterly* 6(3):237–54.

Glick Schiller, Nina, Stephen Crystal, and Denver Lewellen. 1994. "Risky Business: The Cultural Construction of AIDS Risk Groups." *Social Science and Medicine* 38(10):1337–46.

Goffman, Erving. 1961. *Asylums: Essays on the Social Situation of Mental Patients and Other Inmates.* New York: Anchor Books.

Goldberg, Jeffrey. 1994. "The Decline of Upper West Side Civilization." *New York Magazine* 27(17):36–42.

Golden, Stephanie. 1992. *The Women Outside: Meanings and Myths of Homelessness.* Berkeley: University of California Press.

Goldfinger, Stephen M., Ezra Susser, and Brenda Roche. 1994. "HIV, Homelessness, and Serious Mental Illness: Implications for Policy and Practice." Center for Mental Health Services. Rockville, Md.: Department of Health and Human Services.

Golub, Erica L. 1993. "The Female Condom: STD Protection in the Hands of Women." *American Journal of Gynecologic Health* 7(4):91/9–92/10.

Golub, Erica L., and Zena Stein. 1992. "Nonoxynol-9 and the Reduction of HIV Transmission in Women." *AIDS* 6(6):599–600.

———. 1993. "The New Female Condom–Item One on a Woman's AIDS Prevention Agenda." *American Journal of Public Health* 83:498–500.

Gordon, Linda. 1994. *Pitied but Not Entitled: Single Mothers and the History of Welfare.* New York: Free Press.

Gounis, Kostas. 1995. "Ethical Dilemmas in Ethnographic Research on Homelessness." Paper presented at the HIV Center for Clinical and Behavioral Studies. New York.

Gramsci, Antonio. 1971. *Selections from the Prison Notebooks.* New York: International Publishers.

Green, Mark. 1997. *From Welfare to Work: Getting Lost along the Way.* Public Advocate of the City of New York (July).

Greenhouse, Steven. 1998. "Many Participants in Workfare Take the Place of City Workers." *New York Times.* April 13.

Gregory, Steven, and Roger Sanjek, eds. 1994. *Race.* New Brunswick, N.J.: Rutgers University Press.

Hall, Stuart. 1992. "Race, Culture, and Communications: Looking Backward and Forward at Cultural Studies." *Rethinking Marxism* 5(1):10–18.

Harvey David. 1973. *Social Justice and the City.* London: Edward Arnold.

———. 1985. *The Urbanization of Capital.* Oxford: Basil Blackwell.

———. 1989. *The Urban Experience.* Baltimore: Johns Hopkins University Press.

Hebdige, Dick. 1993. "From Culture to Hegemony." In *The Cultural Studies Reader,* ed. Simon During. London: Routledge.

Henwood, Doug. 1997. "Trash-O-Nomics." *In White Trash: Race and Class in America,* ed. Matt Wray and Annalee Newitz. New York: Routledge.

Hernandez, Raymond. 1998a. "Most Dropped from Welfare Don't Get Jobs." *New York Times.* March 23.

———. 1998b. "Agreement Set on Housing of Mentally Ill." *New York Times.* April 10.

Hobsbawm, Eric, and Terence Ranger. 1983. *The Invention of Tradition.* Cambridge: Cambridge University Press.

Hopper, Kim. 1988. "More than Passing Strange: Homelessness and Mental Illness in New York City." *American Ethnologist* 15(1): 155–67.

———. 1991. "Some Old Questions for the New Cross-Cultural Psychiatry." *Medical Anthropology Quarterly* 5(4):299–330.

Hopper, Kim, Ezra Susser, and Sarah Conover. 1986. "Economies of Makeshift: Deindustrialization and Homelessness in New York City." *Urban Anthropology* 14:183–236.

Hwang, Stephen W., E. John Orav, and James J. O'Connell. 1997. "Causes of Death in Homeless Adults in Boston." *Annals of Internal Medicine* 126 (8):625–28.

Ignatieff, Michael. 1985. *The Needs of Strangers: An Essay on Privacy, Solidarity, and the Politics of Being Human.* New York: Viking Penguin.

———. 1993. *Blood and Belonging: Journeys into the New Nationalism.* New York: Farrar, Straus and Giroux.

Institute of Medicine. 1988. *Homelessness, Health and Human Needs.* Washington, D.C.: National Academy Press.

Jencks, Christopher. 1994a. "The Homeless." *New York Review of Books.* April 21: 20–27.

———. 1994b. "Housing the Homeless." *New York Review of Books.* May 12: 39–46.

Jencks, Christopher, and Paul Peterson, eds. 1991. *The Urban Underclass.* Washington, D.C.: Brookings.

Johnson, Bruce D. 1980. "Towards a Theory of Drug Subcultures." In *Theories on Drug Abuse: Selected Contemporary Perspectives,* ed. Dan J. Lettieri, Mollie Sayers, and Helen W. Pearson. Rockville, Md.: National Institute on Drug Abuse.

Jones, Delmos J., Joan Turner, and Joan Montbach. 1992. "Declining Social Services and the Threat to Social Reproduction: An Urban Dilemma." *City and Society* 6(2):99–114.

Kane, Stephanie. 1993. "National Discourse and the Dynamics of

Risk: Ethnography and AIDS Intervention." *Human Organization* 52:224–28.

Katz, Michael B. 1989. *The Undeserving Poor: From the War on Poverty to the War on Welfare.* New York: Pantheon.

———. 1995. *Improving Poor People: The Welfare State, the "Underclass," and Urban Schools as History.* Princeton: Princeton University Press.

Kennedy, Randy. 1997. "Doors that Offer Hope May Shut: A Program That Has Housed the Mentally Ill Lapses." *New York Times.* October 4.

Kernberg, Otto, F. 1984. *Severe Personality Disorders: Psychotherapeutic Strategies.* New Haven: Yale University Press.

Khan, Aisha. 1995. "Homeland, Motherland: Authenticity, Legitimacy, and Ideologies of Place among Muslims in Trinidad." In *Nation and Migration: The Politics of Space in the South Asian Diaspora,* ed. Peter van der Veer. Philadelphia: University of Pennsylvania Press.

Kilborn, Peter T. 1996. "Shrinking Safety Net Cradles Hearts and Hopes of Children." *New York Times.* November 30.

Kleinman, Arthur, and Joan Kleinman. 1991. "Suffering and Its Professional Transformation: Toward an Ethnography of Interpersonal Experience." *Culture, Medicine, and Psychiatry* 15:275–301.

Kleinman, Arthur, Veena Das and Margaret Lock. 1996: "Introduction." *Daedalus* 125(1):xi–xx.

Kozol, Jonathan. 1991. *Savage Inequalities: Children in America's Schools.* New York: Crown.

Krieger, Nancy, and Sally Zierler. 1995. "Accounting for Health of Women." *Current Issues in Public Health* 1:251–56.

Krueger, Liz, Liz Accles, and Laura Wernick. 1997. *Workfare: The Real Deal II.* New York: Community Resource Center, Inc. Access to Benefits Project.

Kurth, Ann, ed. 1993. *Until the Cure: Caring for Women with HIV.* New Haven: Yale University Press.

Lazere, Edward. 1997. *The Poverty Despite Work Handbook.* Washington, D.C.: Center on Budget and Policy Priorities.

Leacock, Eleanor Burke. 1971. *The Culture of Poverty: A Critique.* New York: Simon and Schuster.

Leete, Laura, and Neil Bania. 1997. *The Impact of Welfare Reform on Local Labor Markets.* Cleveland, Ohio: Center on Urban Poverty and Social Change, Case Western Reserve University (July).

Legislative Bulletin 104–32. *The President Signs H.R. 3734, the Personal Responsibility and Work Opportunity Reconciliation Act of 1996.* August 22, 1996. (www.ssa.gov/welfare/legis_bu.html)

Lewis, Oscar. 1966. "The Culture of Poverty." *Scientific American* 215(4):19–25.

Lieberman, Trudy. 1998. "Hunger in America." *The Nation.* March 30: 11–16.

Liebow, Elliot. 1993. *Tell Them Who I Am: The Lives of Homeless Women.* New York: Free Press.

Lindenbaum, Shirley, and Margaret Lock, eds. *1993. Knowledge, Power, and Practice: The Anthropology of Medicine and Everyday Life.* Berkeley: University of California Press.

Link, Bruce G., Ezra Susser, Ann Stueve, Jo Phelan, Robert E. Moore, and Elmer Streuning. 1994. "Lifetime and Five-Year Prevalence of Homelessness in the United States." *American Journal of Public Health* 84(12):1907–12.

Lorde, Audre. 1984. *Sister Outsider.* Traumansburg, N.Y.: Crossing Press.

Maguire, Kathleen, and Timothy J. Flanagan, eds. 1991. *Sourcebook of Criminal Justice Statistics 1990.* U.S. Department of Justice, Bureau of Justice Statistics. Washington, D.C.: USGPO.

Martin, Emily. 1987. *The Woman in the Body: A Cultural Analysis of Reproduction.* Boston: Beacon.

Mathieu, Arline. 1993. "The Medicalization of Homelessness and the Theater of Repression." *Medical Anthropology Quarterly* 7(2):170–84.

Maynard, David. 1995. "Circuits of Capital Accumulation in the Inner City: Theorizing and Contextualizing Urban Ethnography." Paper presented at the American Anthropological Association. Washington, D.C. (November).

Moynihan, Daniel Patrick. 1986. *Family and Nation.* San Diego: Harcourt Brace Jovanovich.

Mullings, Leith P. 1994. "Race, Inequality, and Transformation: Building on the Work of Eleanor Leacock." *Identities* 1(1): 123–29.

Mullings, Leith P., ed. 1987. *Cities of the United States: Studies in Urban Anthropology.* New York: Columbia University Press.

New York City Coalition against Hunger. 1997. *Breadlines in Boomtown: Volunteer Programs Buckle under Growing Need.* New York.

Odets, Walt. 1994. "AIDS Education and Harm Reduction for Gay Men: Psychological Approaches for the 21st Century." *AIDS and Public Policy Journal* 9:1–15.

———. 1995. *In the Shadow of the Epidemic: Being HIV-Negative in the Age of AIDS.* Durham, N.C.: Duke University Press.

Ollman, Bertell. 1979. *Social and Sexual Revolution: Essays on Marx and Reich.* Boston: South End.

O'Neill, Hugh, Kathryn Garcia, and Kathyrn McCormick. 1997. *Where the Jobs Are: How Labor Market Conditions in the New York Area Will Affect the Employment Prospects of Public Assistance Recipients.* New York: Community Service Society.

Pang, Fred. 1996. "Quality People: Lifeblood of a Quality Force." Prepared Statement by the Assistant Secretary of Defense to the Personnel Committee, Senate Armed Services Committee, March 20.

Passaro, Joanne. 1996. *The Unequal Homeless: Men on the Street, Women in Their Place.* New York: Routledge.

Piven, Frances Fox, and Richard A. Cloward. 1971. *Regulating the Poor: The Functions of Public Welfare.* New York: Vintage.

Price, Laurie J. 1992. "A Medical Anthropologist's Ruminations on NIH Funding." *Medical Anthropology Quarterly* 6(2):128–46.

Rapp, Rayna. 1995. "Risky Business: Genetic Counseling in a Shifting World." In *Articulating Hidden Histories: Exploring the Influence of Eric R. Wolf.* ed. Jane Schneider and Rayna Rapp. Berkeley: University of California Press.

Reed, Adolph. 1991. "The Underclass Myth." *Progressive* 55:18–20.

Reiss, Josh, Janet Duni, Dena Lynn Chen, Barbara Keller, Alla Kuznetsova, Dennis McNerney, Tanya Northman, Sarah Ragan, David Randall, Bonnie Siegal, Susan Smith, Gwi-Yop Son, and Nancy Degnan. 1993. *Siting Human Service Facilities: Assessment and Recommendations for Manhattan's Community Board 7.* New York: School of International and Public Affairs, Columbia University.

Roberts, Cokie, and Steven V. Roberts. 1998. "Hunger: A Startling Crisis." *USA Weekend,* March 27–29, 4–7.

Rodriguez Bill, ed. 1994. "Women, Poverty and AIDS: An Introduction." In *Critical Perspectives in Health and Social Justice.* Cambridge, Mass.: Institute for Health and Social Justice.

Rosenberg, Philip S. 1995. "Scope of the AIDS Epidemic in the United States." *Science* 270:1372–75.

Rosenberg, Terry J. 1995. *Updated Poverty Tables for New York City with March 1994 Current Population Survey Estimates.* New York: Community Service Society.

Sack, Kevin. 1995. "Pataki, in Switch, Seeks Cuts in Programs for the Mentally Ill." *New York Times.* March 21.

Said, Edward W. 1995. *The Politics of Dispossession. The Struggle for Palestinian Self-Determination, 1969–1994.* New York: Vintage.

Sanjek, Roger, ed. 1990. *Fieldnotes: The Makings of Anthropology.* Ithaca: Cornell University Press.

Sarasohn, David. 1997. "Hunger on Main Street. Food Banks Are Straining, but the Worst Is Yet to Come." *The Nation.* December 8: 13–18.

Sassen, Saskia. 1991. *The Global City. New York, London, Tokyo.* Princeton: Princeton University Press.

———. 1996a. "Analytic Borderlands: Race, Gender, and Representation in the New City." In *Re-Presenting the City: Ethnicity, Capital, and Culture in the 21st Century Metropolis,* ed. Anthony D. King. Washington Square: New York University Press.

———. 1996b. "Rebuilding the Global City: Economy, Ethnicity, and Space." In *Re-Presenting the City: Ethnicity, Capital, and Culture in the 21st Century Metropolis,* ed. Anthony D. King. Washington Square: New York University Press.

Schneider, Beth E., and Nancy E. Stoller. 1995. *Women Resisting AIDS: Feminist Strategies of Empowerment.* Philadelphia: Temple University Press.

Schneider, Jane. 1995. "Introduction: The Analytic Strategies of Eric R. Wolf." In *Articulating Hidden Histories: Exploring the Influence of Eric R. Wolf,* ed. Jane Schneider and Rayna Rapp. Berkeley: University of California Press.

Schussheim, Morton J. 1987. "Housing Problems and Policies." Congressional Research Service. Washington, D.C.: Library of Congress.

Schwendinger, Herman, and Julia Schwendinger. 1992. Review of *Gimme Shelter,* by Gregg Barak. *Social Justice* 19(1):144–49.

Sennett, Richard, and Jonathan Cobb. 1972. *The Hidden Injuries of Class.* New York: Norton.

Singer, Merrill. 1992. "Biomedicine and the Political Economy of Science." *Medical Anthropology Quarterly* 6:400–404.

———. 1993. "Knowledge for Use: Anthropology and Community-Centered Substance Abuse Research." *Social Science and Medicine* 37:15–26.

————. 1994. "Community-Centered Praxis: Toward an Alternative Non-dominative Applied Anthropology." *Human Organization* 53(4):336–44.

Singer, Merrill, and Hans Baer. 1994. *Critical Medical Anthropology.* Amityville, N.Y.: Baywood.

Smith, Neil. 1996. "After Tompkins Square Park: Degentrification and the Revanchist City." In *Re-Presenting the City: Ethnicity, Capital, and Culture in the 21st Century Metropolis,* ed. Anthony D. King. Washington Square: New York University Press.

Snow, David A., and Leon Anderson. 1993. *Down on Their Luck: A Study of Homeless Street People.* Berkeley: University of California Press.

Stack, Carol. 1974. *All Our Kin.* New York: Harper and Row.

Stafford , Walter W. 1985. *Closed Labor Markets: Underrepresentation of Blacks, Hispanics and Women in New York City's Core Industries and Jobs.* New York: Community Service Society.

Steadman, Henry J., Edward P. Mulvey, John Monahan, Pamela Clark Robbins, Paul Applebaum, Thomas Grisso, Loren H. Roth, and Eric Silver. 1998. "Violence by People Discharged from Acute Psychiatric Inpatient Facilities and by Others in the Same Neighborhoods." *Archives of General Psychiatry* 55:1–9.

Stein, Zena. 1990. "HIV Prevention: The Need for Methods Women Can Use." *American Journal of Public Health* 80:460–62.

————. 1993. "HIV Prevention: An Update on the Status of Methods Women Can Use." *American Journal of Public Health* 83: 1379–82.

————. 1995. "Editorial: More on Women and the Prevention of HIV Infection." *American Journal of Public Health* 85:1485–88.

Stern, Mark. 1984. "The Emergence of the Homeless as a Public Problem." *Social Services Review* 58:291–301.

Stewart D. L., C. J. Zuckerman, and J. M. Ingle. 1994. "HIV Seroprevalence in a Chronically Mentally Ill Population." *Journal of the American Medical Association* 86:519–23.

Stone, Michael E. 1993. *Shelter Poverty: New Ideas on Housing Affordability.* Philadelphia: Temple University Press.

Sugarmann, Josh. 1993. *In Historic First, Saturday Night Special Manufacturer Tops U.S. Domestic Pistol Manufacturers.* Washington, D.C.:Violence Policy Center.

————. N.d. "Reverse FIRE." MOJO Wire. Available at <www.motherjones.com>

Susser Ezra, E. Valencia, and J. Torres. 1994. "A Curriculum for HIV

Prevention among Homeless Mentally Ill Men." *Psychosocial Rehabilitation Journal* 17:31–40.

Susser Ezra, E. Valencia, M. Miller, W. Y. Tsai, H. F. L. Meyer-Bahlburg, and S. Conover. 1995. "Sexual Behavior of Homeless Men at Risk for HIV." *American Journal of Psychiatry* 152: 583–87.

Susser, Ezra, E. Valencia, P. Colson, H. F. L. Meyer-Bahlburg, R. Schilling, A. Felix, and K. Gounis. 1992. *Critical Time Intervention to Reduce HIV Risk Behaviors among Mentally Ill Individuals.* New York: HIV Center for Clinical and Behavioral Studies.

Susser, Ezra, Elie Valencia, Sarah Conover, Alan Felix, Wei-Yann Tsai, and Richard Jed Wyatt. 1997. "Preventing Recurrent Homelessness among Mentally Ill Men: A 'Critical Time' Intervention after Discharge from a Shelter." *American Journal of Public Health* 87:2:256–62.

Susser, Ezra, Eliecer Valencia, and Sarah Conover. 1993. "Prevalence of HIV Infection among Psychiatric Patients in a New York City Men's Shelter." *American Journal of Public Health* 83(4): 568–70.

Susser, Ida. 1982. *Norman Street: Poverty and Politics in an Urban Neighborhood.* New York: Oxford University Press.

———. 1996. "The Construction of Poverty and Homelessness in U.S. Cities." *Annual Review of Anthropology* 25:411–35.

Treichler, Paula A. 1988. "AIDS, Gender, and Biomedical Discourse: Current Contests for Meaning." In *AIDS: The Burdens of History,* ed. Elizabeth Fee and Daniel M. Fox. Berkeley: University of California Press.

Tynes, L. Lee, Frederic J. Sautter, Barbara E. McDermott, and Daniel K. Winstead. 1993. "Risk of HIV Infection in the Homeless and Chronically Mentally Ill." *Southern Medical Journal* 86(3): 276–81.

Uchitelle, Louis. 1997. "The Shift toward Self-Reliance in the Welfare System." *New York Times.* January 13.

U.S. Bureau of the Census. 1990. *Population Characteristics, Manhattan Community District 7.* Washington, D.C.: Bureau of the Census.

———. 1996. *Statistical Abstract of the United States.* Washington, D.C.: Bureau of the Census.

"Use of Soup Kitchens Is Found to Be Increasing." 1998. *New York Times.* February 15.

Valentine, Charles A. 1968. *Culture and Poverty: Critique and Counter-Proposals.* Chicago: University of Chicago Press.

Van Vugt, Johannes P., ed. 1994. *AIDS Prevention and Services: Community Based Research.* Westport, Conn.: Bergin and Garvey.

Volavka, J., A. Concit, P. Czobor, R. Douyon, J. O'Donnell, and F. Ventura. 1991. "HIV Seroprevalence and Risk Behaviors in Psychiatric Inpatients." *Psychiatric Research* 39:109–14.

Wallace, Rodrick. 1990. "Urban Desertification, Public Health, and Public Order: 'Planned Shrinkage,' Violent Death, Substance Abuse, and AIDS in the Bronx." *Social Science and Medicine* 31: 801–13.

———. 1993. "Social Disintegration and the Spread of AIDS-II: Meltdown of Sociogeographic Structure in Urban Minority Neighborhoods." *Social Science and Medicine* 37:887–96.

Waterston Alisse. 1993. *Street Addicts in the Political Economy.* Philadelphia: Temple University Press.

———. 1997. "Anthropological Research and the Politics of HIV Prevention: Towards a Critique of Policy and Priorities in the Age of AIDS." *Social Science and Medicine* 44 (9):1381–91.

———. 1998. "Doing Our Home Work: Anthropologists on Homelessness and Housing in the United States." *American Anthropologist* 100 (1):12–15.

———. 1998. "The Facts of the Matter: Consequences of Welfare 'Reform' for Poor Women in the United States." Paper presented at the American Anthropological Association, Philadelphia (December).

Weitzman, Phillip. 1989. *Worlds Apart: Housing, Race/Ethnicity and Income in New York City, 1978–1987.* New York: Community Service Society.

Williams, Brett. 1988. *Upscaling Downtown.* Ithaca, N.Y.: Cornell University Press.

———. 1992. "Poverty among African Americans in the Urban United States." *Human Organization* 51(2):164–74.

———. 1994. "Babies and Banks: The 'Reproductive Underclass' and the Raced, Gendered Masking of Debt." In *Race,* ed. Steven Gregory and Roger Sanjek. New Brunswick, N.J.: Rutgers University Press.

———. 1996. "'There Goes the Neighborhood': Gentrification, Displacement, and Homelessness in Washington, D.C." In *There's No Place Like Home: Anthropological Perspectives on Housing and Homelessness in the United States,* ed. Anna Lou Dehavenon. Westport, Conn.: Bergin and Garvey.

Williams, Terry. 1989. *The Cocaine Kids.* Reading, Pa.: Addison-Wesley.

Wilson, William J. 1987. *The Truly Disadvantaged.* Chicago: University of Chicago Press.

———. 1989. "The Underclass: Issues, Perspectives, and Public Policy." *Annals of the American Academy of Political and Social Sciences* 501:182–92.

Wolch, Jennifer R., and Stacy Rowe. 1992. "On the Streets: Mobility Paths of the Urban Homeless." *City and Society* 6(2): 115–40.

Wolch, Jennifer R., and Michael Dear. 1993. *Malign Neglect: Homelessness in an American City.* San Francisco: Jossey-Bass.

Wolf, Eric R. 1982. *Europe and the People without History.* Berkeley: University of California Press.

———. 1990. "Distinguished Lecture: Facing Power: Old Insights, New Questions." *American Anthropologist* 92(3):586–96.

Wright, James D. 1995. "Ten Essential Observations on Guns in America." American Firearms Council, Atlanta. Available at <www.assc.org>

Young, Iris M. 1994. "Gender as Seriality: Thinking about Women as a Social Collective." *Signs* 19(3):713–38.

Zepezauer, Mark, and Arthur Naiman. 1996. *Take the Rich Off Welfare.* Tucson, Ariz.: Odonian.

Zylan, Yvonne. 1996. "Comment on Fraser and Gordon's 'A Genealogy of Dependency: Tracing a Keyword of the U.S. Welfare State.'" *Signs* 21(2):515–30.

Index